Tips and Traps When Negotiating Real Estate

Other McGraw-Hill Books by Robert Irwin

Tips and Traps When Buying a Home

Tips and Traps When Selling a Home

Tips and Traps When Buying a Co-Op, Condo, or Townhouse

Tips and Traps for Making Money in Real Estate

Tips and Traps When Renovating Your Home

Tips and Traps for New Home Owners

Tips and Traps When Building Your Home

Tips and Traps When Mortgage Hunting

How to Find Hidden Real Estate Bargains

How to Buy a Home When You Can't Afford It

How to Get Started in Real Estate Investing

How to Invest in Real Estate with Little or No Money Down

Home Buyer's Checklist

Home Seller's Checklist

Home Renovation Checklist

Home Closing Checklist

Buy, Rent, and Sell

Tips and Traps When Negotiating Real Estate

Robert Irwin

Second Edition

McGraw-Hill

New York   Chicago   San Francisco   Lisbon   London
Madrid   Mexico City   Milan   New Delhi   San Juan
Seoul   Singapore   Sydney   Toronto

2 3 4 5 6 7 8 9 0   FGR/FGR   0 9 8 7 6

ISBN 0-07-145286-9

McGraw-Hill books are available at special quantity discounts to use as premiums and sales promotions, or for use in corporate training programs. For more information, please write to the Director of Special Sales, McGraw-Hill Professional, Two Penn Plaza, New York, NY 10121-2298. Or contact your local bookstore.

This book is printed on recycled, acid-free paper containing a minimum of 50% recycled, de-inked fiber.

Library of Congress Cataloging-in-Publication Data

Irwin, Robert.
    Tips & traps when negotiating real estate / Robert Irwin.— 2nd ed.
       p.   cm.
    ISBN 0-07-145286-9 (alk. paper)
    1. Real estate business. 2. House buying. 3. House selling. 4. Mortgage loans. 5. Real estate investment. 6. Negotiation in business. I. Title: Tips and traps when negotiating real estate. II. Title.
HD1379.I673   2006
333.33—dc22

                                         2005017830

Contents

1

Negotiating a Successful Deal

Everything in real estate is negotiable. That includes the price, the terms, the appliances, the commission, the light fixtures and, in some strange cases, even the pets!

However, the word *negotiable* is not magic. It doesn't mean you'll always get what you want. If you're a buyer who wants a 15 percent reduction in price, you could get it *if* you're willing to pay cash, do a quick deal, make other concessions, or buy when the market is cold. If you're a seller who insists on getting full price, you could get it *if* the market's hot, or you're willing to loan the buyer money to help make the purchase, or you'll allow the buyer to move in before escrow closes, or make other concessions.

Negotiation is give and take. Of course, what we all want is to be able to give as little and take as much as possible. And, indeed, we'll see just how to do that in this book. However, keep in mind that the best negotiations end with a win–win situation, one in which all parties are happy with the deal.

TIP

Think of negotiating as the art of accomplishing the possible, not the impossible.

The actual rules of negotiating real estate begin in the next chapter. However, I encourage readers to go through the following true story of Sondra and Dana carefully to see negotiating in practice during an actual residential real estate transaction.

Finding the Property

Sondra and Dana owned a home they had purchased a few years earlier in Sacramento, California. The home was only a couple of years old, but it was small (only three bedrooms) for their expanding family. (They had one child, were anticipating a second, and Sondra needed a home office.)

Further, their home was in a tract with a small yard and Dana was the sort who liked to "work the ground." He wanted a bigger tract of land where he could "plant crops" and perhaps have a horse, or even a cow. He wanted a country home rather than a city home.

So they began looking for a new house. And while properties such as the one they wanted were, indeed, available in the area, prices were rising rapidly and Dana felt that his chances of finding one were slim. Nevertheless, for a whole month of weekends, he and Sondra went out looking, being mostly disappointed with what they saw and the prices asked.

Thus, they were both surprised one weekend when an agent showed them a property with four acres of land. The house was not much bigger than the one they currently owned, but it did have an extra bedroom over the garage. It was an old home, but it had been partially remodeled with new air conditioning and an expanded family room. It would need work, but they figured they were up to it.

What Dana really liked, and Sondra tolerated, was the expanse of land that came with the home. True, it was flat with only two old oak trees on it and the rest weeds, but Dana saw all sorts of potential. He envisioned a barn where they could have animals, a field where they could grow vegetables. And he fell in love with the 1941 Ford tractor rusting out back, which he imagined he could get running again.

Making the Initial Offer

There was virtually no discussion over whether they should buy the place. They both knew they wanted it. The only concern was *if* they could buy it.

The asking price was $350,000 for the home. Dana and Sondra saw a mortgage broker who said they could afford the payments on a maximum loan of $325,000 at current interest rates. That left another $25,000 needed for the down payment plus another $7,000 for the buyer's closing costs. However, they figured they had $40,000 equity in their current home, even after paying the seller's transaction costs to sell it, including the commission. Therefore, they should come out okay with even a few dollars to spare.

Their big concern was timing. The property, owned by a couple named Wilson, had only been for sale for a couple of weeks and Sondra and Dana's agent, Madeline, indicated there had been lots of interest in it. She talked to the Wilson's agent, Max, who said several other agents had called to say they anticipated making offers, although none had done so yet. Quick action was needed.

The trouble was that while Sondra and Dana could indeed buy the property, in order to do so they first had to sell their current home and get their money from the sale. That would take weeks, if not a month or more. Yet, to get the Wilson property they needed to make an offer immediately.

Madeline, their agent, suggested making a "contingent" offer.

The Contingent Offer

Madeline explained that a "contingent" offer was one in which the buyers said they would purchase the home, provided they could sell their existing home. The new purchase was contingent on the sale of the old property. If Sondra and Dana couldn't sell their existing home, then they weren't committed to purchase the new property.

Sondra and Dana said that sounded perfect. They were completely protected. Then Dana said, "Now, let's see if we can negotiate the sellers down in price."

Their agent, Madeline, held up her hand. "I don't think so," she said.

She pointed out that a contingent offer was a *weak* one. "You're asking the sellers to agree to wait to sell their home until you first sell yours. If you can't sell, they've waited for nothing. In effect, you're asking them now to worry about the sale of two properties instead of one."

"That's asking a lot of the sellers, isn't it?" said Dana.

"Yes, it is," replied Madeline. "And if you want to get your deal, you have to give them a reason to go along. If you now try to cut their price, you're asking them to make two major concessions—one the contingency, and two the price cut. Maybe in a very slow market they might accept. But the market here has been very hot, there are a lot of lookers, and their agent said they were expecting other offers momentarily.

"Therefore, in order to get the deal, my suggestion is that you come in at full price. Or, perhaps, even over the asking price!"

Dana looked askance. "I can't imagine offering more than full price. Particularly since we're offering them a cash deal. We'll come up with a cash down payment on a new loan, which means all cash out to them. That's a good deal for them."

Madeline nodded. "Yes, it is. Perhaps we can get it for full price. But, keep in mind that over the past few months in this hot market, many properties are selling for thousands over the asking price. Getting them to accept will be a close thing." Dana and Sondra nodded, and Madeline drew up the full price contingent offer.

TIP

When negotiating, it's important to see not only your own perspective, but the other side's as well. Always be ready to give up something to get something. Just be sure that you don't mind what you're giving up, and that you really want what you're getting.

Pushing the Time Line

Madeline presented the offer and reported back that the sellers understood it, but weren't too happy about it. They said they wanted to take a few days to think about it. She said she was worried, however, because the seller's agent, Max, said that other brokers were calling and saying they were hoping to write up offers very soon. It didn't look good.

Dana got on the phone and asked Madeline if there was a time limit on their offer. Madeline replied, "Yes, I always allow the sellers three full days. It gives them time to come to a decision. It was part of the offer you signed."

Dana rubbed his forehead, told Madeline to hold for a moment, and looked at Sondra. He said, "We're going to lose the property. While we're giving the sellers days to decide, other brokers will come in with offers that probably won't be contingent. The sellers will probably accept the first full-price offer they receive that's non-contingent. And we'll lose out."

TRAP

Offers must be presented to sellers as they are received, even if the sellers are in the process of considering an earlier offer. Agents who wait to present a second offer while the sellers are considering a first one are not living up to their fiduciary responsibilities.

"You're right," said Sondra. "Tell Madeline to communicate to the sellers that we'll give them until 6:00 tonight to sign; otherwise our offer is off."

Dana looked at his watch. "It's already 3:00 in the afternoon," he said.

"Right," said Sondra. "Either they accept our offer right now, or we'll look elsewhere. We don't want to give them time to wait for a better offer to come in."

TIP

Time is the essence of any negotiation. Either you make it work for you, or it works against you.

Dana told Madeline what they wanted, and she protested that their offer had already given the sellers three days.

Dana said, "We can withdraw our offer any time before they sign, right?" Madeline agreed they had that right.

"Well, then give them until 6:00 tonight. Tell them we're looking at other properties, which we are. If they don't accept, we'll pull the offer."

Madeline said she didn't like being so harsh with sellers. But Dana insisted, so she said she'd do what she could. She called back an hour later and said she and Max were going to meet with the sellers at 5:00 to see what could be done.

Sondra and Dana sat by the phone and it rang at precisely 6:00. It was Madeline. She said, "They signed. You've got your new home!"

TRAP

 Some agents don't like the pressure of tough negotiating. If that's the case, then either demand that your agent perform to your desires or get a new agent.

Sondra and Dana cheered. Then Madeline said, "They made a few changes and I'll be right over to have you sign them."

"What changes?" asked Dana.

"Very little," Madeline said. "I'll explain them when I get there," and she hung up.

By 7:00, Madeline was there. The sellers had added two new conditions to the sales agreement. The first was that they had raised the price by $5,000. The second was that they gave Sondra and Dana a maximum of 30 days to find a buyer for their existing home.

Sondra said, "I think we can sell the property under those conditions. But, I don't want to pay any more than the asking price for the property."

Dana looked at her and said, "But, it's in the agreement they signed."

"Too bad," said Sondra. "It's not in the agreement we signed."

TIP

 Whenever there's a counteroffer that differs in any way from the original offer, it has to be considered as an entirely new offer. You're not committed to accept anything you didn't sign for.

Dana looked at Madeline, who looked worried. "Do we have to accept the additional $5,000 in price?" he asked.

Madeline shook her head, "Only if you want to buy the property. I talked to those sellers until I was blue in the face, but the only way they will accept the contingency is if you come up with more money. I don't believe they'll budge another inch.

"Besides, Max says that another agent wants to come in and present an offer at 9:00 this evening. You've only got until then to agree to what the sellers want. That's their time limit."

TRAP

What makes negotiating tricky is the threat of the competing offer. If the sellers have only you, then you can hold out for a better deal. But if others are competing to buy, then your position is weaker. Similarly, if you have other properties you're considering as a buyer, your position is stronger than if you have only the one you're bidding on.

Sondra and Dana asked to be excused and went into their bedroom to discuss it by themselves. Sondra said that she thought having to pay more than the asking price was a rip-off.

Dana wasn't so sure. He said that prices of properties were appreciating rapidly in the area, more than 15 percent the previous year. Further, in a month of looking this was the only property they had found; hence they didn't have any alternative property to make an offer on. Finally, with prices going up, if they didn't get this house, they might be priced right out of the market.

"But," Dana said, "the crucial thing is the other offer. I don't think our agent, Madeline, is the best negotiator, but I think she's honest. I'm sure that Max, the seller's agent, did say there was another offer coming in. And if he told her, he told the sellers. And if that's the case, I doubt they'll budge, at least until they see the other offer. And even if it's for just the full price, not the additional $5,000, *with no contingency*, they'll take it. I would."

Sondra nodded. It made sense.

They came back out and told Madeline they would pay $5,000 more. She breathed a sigh of relief, took out her cell phone, and immediately called Max, who was waiting with the sellers, to tell him that the buyers had accepted. They had a deal.

Once the acceptance of an offer (or, in this case, a counteroffer) without changes is communicated to the other party, it's a nearly complete transaction. Of course, the paperwork must always be signed and quickly delivered to all parties. In real estate, according to the Statute of Frauds, no sales agreement can be made verbally.

Complications

Sondra and Dana immediately put their home up for sale. They listed it with Madeline, who said she would give them a break on the commission since she was getting two deals out of it. They compared five other homes very similar to theirs that had sold in the past three months and selected a price that was just slightly below the average price of the other homes. They wanted a quick sale and were, hopefully, pricing it right.

Sondra and Dana immediately went through a major cleaning of their home. They painted the front, touched up the walls inside, cleaned the carpets, had a crew come in to do a thorough job on the kitchen and baths, and trimmed and mowed the yard. "We've got to get this sold—fast!" Dana said.

The first weekend, Madeline held an Open House and dozens of people came by. Many seemed interested, but none made an offer.

The second weekend, Madeline held a "caravan" at the house, in which other agents both from her office and other offices came by to look at the property. Madeline told Sondra and Dana that getting the word out to other agents was the best way to get a sale.

The third weekend, Madeline held another Open House, and when the final lookers left, she appeared worried. She said, "We haven't had any offers. I think you should drop your price."

Sondra shook her head. "We've looked at comparable sales and our house is priced fairly. Besides, we paid over asking price for our new home. Why should we accept under market price for this one?"

"Because," Madeline said, "you want a quick sale."

Sondra looked at Dana and he shook his head. "I'm with you on this one," he replied. "If we can't sell this house for a fair price, then why even bother looking for another one? We'll just stay here.

Besides, I don't think cutting the price now will make that big a difference, since our price is already slightly below market. It must just be that the right buyer hasn't come by yet."

TIP

Dropping your price will always attract more buyers, but usually they are the ones looking for a bargain, who will tend to make even lower lowball offers.

"Anyhow," added Sondra, "we need to get our asking price in order to have enough cash to buy the new property and pay for the move." Madeline left looking even more worried.

By the fourth week, as their contingency was ready to expire, Sondra and Dana sat down to talk it out. "We gave it our best shot," he said. She nodded and held his hand. "There will be other houses. We'll relist with another agent and take our time. After we sell, then we'll go looking again."

TRAP

The question of whether to sell first or buy first is a big one. In a hot market where prices are moving up rapidly, it's often best to lock in the price of the new home before selling the old. In a cold market where prices are steady, it usually works best the other way.

On the last day of their contingency, Madeline called to say she had an offer, a "full price" offer! She was coming right down to show it to them.

She arrived half an hour later by herself. She said the buyer's agent didn't have time to come by. But she could explain the offer perfectly well. The name of the buyers was Love . . . and it was a contingency offer!

Sondra and Dana were flabbergasted. The Loves, the would-be buyers of their home, wanted them to sign a contingency giving the Loves 30 days to sell their own home. The Loves were doing to them, what they had done to the Wilsons!

However, Madeline reported that the Loves' broker said that he thought he might have a buyer and the house might sell within a week.

"It's like musical chairs," said Sondra. "We can't buy until we sell. And our buyers can't purchase until they sell."

"We can't do it," said Dana. "We're on the last day of our own contingency. The Wilsons expect us to be ready to go today."

"I know," said Madeline. "It will take some arm twisting, but now that you have a sale, I think the Wilsons will be willing to give you an extension. At least it's worth a try. What do you have to lose?"

Sondra looked at Dana and they both nodded. So they signed first, making sure that the new agreement was tied to the old. It gave the buyers of their existing home, the Loves, 30 days to sell, provided the sellers of their new home, the Wilsons, gave Sondra and Dana an additional 30 days.

Madeline drove off and called them an hour later. She was at the Wilson home, and she was having trouble. The Wilsons were already half moved out, having assumed the deal would soon close. Now they were angry about the delay. They wanted an additional $5,000 to compensate them for their troubles. Madeline said she was writing up the new extension and would be right over.

Dana told her to hold on for a moment while he explained it to Sondra. Sondra said, "If they're already half moved out, then it will be even more difficult for them if they have to start over, put their home back on the market, and wait for a new buyer. And even after they find that new buyer, which could take weeks, they'll have to wait another 30 days or more for the deal to close. We still offer them the fastest deal, particularly now that our house has sold. We're in a better position than Madeline thinks. I don't believe we should agree to pay an additional $5,000."

TIP

It's important to know when to stick to your guns. As in poker, if you have the winning hand, you don't want to fold or back down on a bet.

Dana got back on the phone and explained to Madeline what his wife had said. He then told her, "Tell them that we're within the terms of our original agreement. We found a buyer for our home within 30 days. It's just going to take a bit longer to close the deal. We already gave them an additional $5,000 for the contingency. We don't feel we should have to pay for it twice. And we won't."

Madeline said it wouldn't fly, but she'd try. She called back half an hour later saying the Wilsons had agreed. They were a nice older couple and really wanted Sondra and Dana to have their home, so they were willing to wait an additional 30 days. But they were moving out over the weekend. She'd be right over with the changes for Sondra and Dana to sign.

TIP

It's important to know what motivates the other party to a negotiation. If you can show them how doing it your way is to their advantage, they might just go along.

The New Sale

Madeline called a week later and said that the Loves, the buyers of Dana and Sondra's home, had already found their own buyer, a *noncontingent* buyer. She was trying to hurry the sale and, hopefully, within a few weeks the Love's new buyer would have a new mortgage, purchase the home, and then, like dominoes, the other deals would follow along. She told them to get ready to move. In fact, the Wilsons had already moved out. Madeline said she could get permission for them to start putting their things in their new home. She said, "You want to be ready to move as soon as all the deals close. This way you can get a head start on moving in."

Dana asked Madeline if there were any problems with any of the deals that she could foresee. "None," she replied. "The Loves, buyers of your old home, had a preapproval letter, so they should get their financing. And so do the buyers of their home. It should all go quickly, now."

Dana hung up and shook his head. "Too many things have already gone wrong. If we move our furniture and boxes into the new house and, for some reason, the buyers of our old home don't

go through with the deal, we'll have to move them back. Better wait
and see."

TRAP

 Try not to back yourself into a corner. When negotiating, you never want to be forced to move forward
because you've lost the opportunity to move back.

Dana and Sondra waited as patiently as they could for news, and
three weeks later almost to the day, Madeline called and said that
the Loves, the buyers of their house, were ready to sign the papers.
It would, indeed, work just like dominoes.

It would all transpire almost simultaneously; each of the three
buyers would sign loan documents. And each of the three sellers
would sign their deeds and closing instructions. The money would
flow from the buyers' of the Loves' home to the Loves. The Loves
would transfer the money to Sondra and Dana, buying their home.
And Dana and Sondra would then transfer the money to the
Wilsons, buying the four acres. In a matter of hours it would all be
over.

Sondra and Dana went to their escrow company, signed dozens of
papers, and then went home. The Loves, who were buying Sondra
and Dana's existing house, called and asked if they could be out
early the next day, since they wanted to move in.

Dana said he was still suspicious. What if things didn't go as
planned? What if they let the Loves move into their old house and
they moved into the Wilson place, their new house. If the deals didn't
close, suddenly they'd be renting their new house and they'd have the
Loves as tenants in their old one!

So he told the Loves he wouldn't move until all the escrows had
closed and all the deeds had been recorded. The Loves sounded
angry.

A few minutes later, Dana and Sondra got a call from Madeline,
their agent. She said they had to be out to be sure that the whole
thing didn't fall apart. The Loves were threatening not to sign
unless they knew that Dana and Sondra would be out of the house.
"You don't want to lose out on the new house you're buying by

refusing to leave your old home in a timely fashion, do you?" Madeline asked.

Dana looked at Sondra and she nodded. He told Madeline, "We're not moving until title is transferred. Until then, this is our house and we're staying here!"

TIP

It's important to know when you're in a strong position . . . and not to budge from it, even when those in weaker positions want you to move.

More Complications

Sondra and Dana waited to hear that title had transferred. They waited a day, two days, three days, five days. Finally, Madeline called and said something had delayed the Loves' getting financing. But now it was all straightened out. Sondra and Dana had to go down to escrow and sign new papers.

"Why?" Sondra asked.

"Because the old loan documents you signed were dated. We simply need to get new dates and new calculations for payouts for the new dates."

Dutifully, Sondra and Dana went down and signed again. And again they waited a day, three days, a week. Then Madeline called and said the Wilsons, whose four-acre house Sondra and Dana were buying, were agitated. The deal had taken too long. They felt they could have rented their place out during all the waiting to make up for the monthly mortgage payments they were still making on an empty home. They wanted $2,000 in lost rent, or else they would simply pull out of the deal since all the deadlines agreed upon had long passed.

Sondra told Madeline to wait, and explained what she had said to Dana. He thought about it and said, "If we pay the money now and the deals never close, we're out $2,000. If we pay and there's a further delay, they'll want even more money. As far as I'm concerned, we should write the whole thing off and begin looking for another house to buy. I don't think it will ever close."

Sondra got back on the phone and told Madeline that not only weren't they paying the $2,000 in rent, they were backing out of the deal. After all, all their deadlines had passed as well.

Madeline said she'd call right back.

TIP

It's important to know when to walk away. As a negotiating maneuver, it puts enormous pressure on the other parties to concede. On the other hand, you have to be willing to lose the deal, because the other parties can likewise say goodbye.

Twenty minutes later, Madeline was back on the phone. She said she had agreed to give the Wilsons half of what they were asking from her own money, $1,000, for another two-week extension. Further, she was going to call the Loves' broker (the people buying Sondra and Dana's house) to see what the problem was and to correct it. Would Sondra and Dana agree to wait another two weeks?

When they agreed, Madeline came right over with another extension for them to sign.

The next day, Sondra called their state's Department of Real Estate and talked to one of the employees. She explained the problem and asked if there was anything that the state could do.

The employee was sympathetic, but said that from what Sondra had explained, it didn't sound as though any of the agents had really done anything wrong. He said that contingent sales were the hardest to close and often ran into lots of problems. He wished Sondra luck and told her to call back if any further more serious problems developed.

The Real Explanation

A few days later, Madeline, their agent, called to say she had found the trouble. The Loves, who were buying Sondra and Dana's house, had a problem. The Loves' house had not passed a termite inspection. Some work needed to be done, which the Loves had agreed to pay for. But no one had ordered the work done—their agent, who should have been tracking the deal, had dropped the ball. And the Loves couldn't sell to their buyers because their buyers' lender wouldn't fund until a termite clearance was ordered. Hence the Loves couldn't sell their home, couldn't buy Sondra and Dana's home, and Sondra and Dana couldn't buy the Wilsons' four acres.

"But, I've called in my own termite exterminator company and am having the work done even as we speak," Madeline said.

Sondra replied, "Surely, you don't expect us to pay for that?!"

"No," Madeline said. I will pay for it. And be compensated when the Wilsons' sale closes. It'll just be a few more days."

When she hung up, Sondra asked Dana, "Do you think we should ask for a few thousand dollars in compensation from the Loves, our buyers, because the deal has dragged on so long? After all, we're still making payments on our old house."

"True," Dana answered, "but we're also still living in it. And while we could ask for compensation, we really don't want more money . . . we want to buy our new home. Just waiting and hoping may be the best bet right now."

TIP

Know what your true goal is. Is it to get compensation for real or imagined damages to you? Or is it to close the deal?

At Last!

Two days later, Madeline called to say that all escrows had closed. They needed to move immediately into their new home.

Once the escrows closed, everything moved like clockwork. Dana and Sondra moved into their new four-acre home. The Loves moved into their old one. And, presumably, the buyers of the Loves' home moved into *it*.

About a week later, on a Saturday, Sondra and Dana were unpacking boxes. Madeline drove up and congratulated them on their new home. She brought them a flowering plant to help celebrate.

Before she left she said, "I was out the $1,000 in rent I paid to the Wilsons to keep the deal alive. Technically, you don't owe it, since you didn't move into the property until the deals closed. But, I was wondering if you would split it with me? After all, it's what made the whole thing happen."

Sondra looked at Dana, who nodded, then said, "That's not entirely correct. The deal would have flowed smoothly *if* the termite work had been done in a timely manner. That was the fault of the Loves, or at least their agent. And by not being right on top of it, indirectly it was also your fault. There's no reason we should pay any money for someone else's mistakes."

Madeline nodded and said she understood. She told them to remember her when they sold, and drove off.

TRAP

Don't let others blame you for mistakes that you didn't cause. Stand up and correct the accusation. Accepting blame is the fastest way to lose money, if not the deal.

Conclusion

No, Sondra and Dana were not Donald Trump, who might have ended up owning all three houses if he had been involved in the deal! But, then again, presumably neither are you.

When negotiating in real estate, it's very important to keep your eye on the donut and not the hole. What Sondra and Dana ultimately wanted was to purchase their dream home. They weren't interested in punishing others for problems caused. They weren't interested in making additional money on the chance of losing the house. They didn't want to profit from someone else's error.

They simply and honestly wanted to move forward. And that's probably the best direction anyone can take.

TIP

Remember the old adage, "What goes around comes around." A win–win situation is always best in the long run.

2
Control Time

As we all know, time passes. It tends to slip away. And unless we're in control of what happens with time, particularly when we're involved in negotiations, it can do us in.

Consider the professional football team that's down by three points in the last two minutes of the game. A good quarterback, one who knows how to "work the clock," as they say in football, will make every second count. He can conceivably maneuver his team down the field and score, tying up the game, or perhaps even winning. But a quarterback who doesn't "stop the clock" soon finds that no matter how well the team is performing, he's run out of time, the game's over, and he has lost.

Football is a metaphor for many things in life, real estate being one of them. How you control the clock in negotiations will, in large part, determine whether you get the deal you want, get a lesser deal, or no deal at all. In fact, the sentence "Time is of the essence" is usually written into most real estate contracts to emphasize its importance.

There are at least four different ways that you, as a buyer, seller, landlord, or tenant, can control time when you're negotiating in real estate. We'll consider all of them.

TIP

Time invested is almost as good as money invested.

Invest in Time

This is a little bit tricky to understand at first, but once you get the hang of it, you'll find it really works. Let's say you want to lease a house. But instead of the customary one-year lease, you want a lease for only six months. And instead of taking the place "as is," you want the owner to paint the entire interior of the house. And you have a dog and three cats . . . and a waterbed.

You get the idea. You've got a whole lot of extras that make you a landlord's nightmare. How do you get the landlord to accept you anyway?

Let's say you walk up to the owner and simply blurt it all out. "I want to rent your house, but you have to repaint it, give me a six-month lease instead of a full year, accept my pets, and allow me to keep a waterbed, which could leak and ruin your property." Now, how do you think the typical landlord is going to react? If it were me, I would show you to the nearest door and not breathe easy until you were long gone. (Just in case you've never been a landlord, the only thing worse than dogs, cats, and waterbeds is tenants who want to stay only a short time.)

On the other hand, let's say you tried a different approach, one involving time. You came to the landlord and indicated you were interested in the property, but you weren't sure. You talked with him a while, not mentioning your "problems," and you got to know one another. Then you left.

Chances are he was favorably impressed by you and, all things being equal, considered you a likely candidate for a tenant. He hoped you'd come back. (Landlords hate showing property to people who have no intention of renting but are just out "shopping," or people the landlord would never want as tenants—it's a complete waste of their time.)

The next day you do come back and you say you're definitely interested. The landlord is going to be pleased. At last he'll get that empty (and costly to maintain while empty) house off his hands. You further add that the rental amount is okay and you have excellent credit, which you'd be more than willing to let the landlord check out. Now the landlord is sure to be delighted. But, you mention, you want to be sure the property is just right. Could he tell you about the neighborhood, the schools, the shopping?

The landlord proceeds to spend the next hour telling you about the marvelous environment around the rental. At the end of that time you appear duly impressed. You mention that you really are interested, but the place seems so dingy. Would he consider repainting it?

The landlord might think to himself that he'd really rather not paint it. He might honestly think that it's probably rentable as is, or else he would already have painted it. On the other hand, during all that time spent talking, he's learned a lot about you. You've effectively presented yourself as a good catch as a tenant. While he would probably have said no if you had just walked up and asked him, now he's going to seriously consider acquiescing. The truth is, the time you and he have spent together has been well spent. Better a bird in the hand than half a dozen in the bush, he may think to himself. A good tenant, after all, is worth a paint job. And now you're seen as that good tenant.

So he agrees to the painting and you say that as a consequence you're quite sure you want it, but you'll be back tomorrow with your husband. You want to make the final decision together. The landlord pretty much figures he's got the deal sewed up and makes arrangements with the painters. You fill out an application and give the landlord permission to check your credit.

Tomorrow you and your husband show up and go through the house all over again. The landlord's now pointing out how much nicer this room or that cabinet will look with new paint on it. He's already accepted repainting and it's no longer an issue. You ask how well the heating system, the air conditioning, the features such as the fireplace, the dishwasher, etc. work. Time drags on. Finally, you say you'll take it. The landlord is very pleased.

However, you say you can only take a six-month lease. The landlord is not pleased. He has assumed all along that you would take a year's lease. He says he really wants to lease the property for a whole year. You nod that you understand, but point out that you're not sure just how long you're going to be in the area. You can only guarantee six months. If things work out, you could stay longer.

The landlord is thinking to himself that he should say no and wait for a tenant who will agree to stay longer. But if he doesn't accept you, he's got to start all over with someone else. Further, by now he's obtained a credit report and knows you're a good risk and probably will take good care of the place. And, he may rationalize, one never knows what will happen after six months. Maybe you'll stay another six months, or even longer. What it comes down to, finally, is whether or not he's going to throw away all the time and effort he's already expended on you . . . when the only problem you offer is a shorter term. (By now, the issue of painting has receded into yesterday's problem.)

TIP

A concession, once made, stops being a concession.

You shake hands with the landlord and sit down to read the rental agreement. After spending some time going through the contract boilerplate, you come to the subject of pets. You say you have several pets that are well behaved. Three are outdoor pets and one is a potty-trained indoor cat. The landlord grits his teeth and writes the number 4 into the contract with regard to pets. He also adds several hundred dollars to the security deposit, to which you happily agree.

Finally, before signing off, he asks if you have a waterbed. You innocently mention that you do, and ask if that's a problem. The landlord shakes his head and says, "I'll have to increase your deposit some more." You sigh and say that it's already high and you're quite sure the waterbed is safe. It has never leaked and is of a special design that simply doesn't get holes. Okay, he says, worn out, and the agreement is signed. You've negotiated the deal you wanted.

Of course, in real life one never knows what any landlord will do. However, the point here is that as more and more time is spent on the negotiations, it becomes increasingly hard for the landlord to dump the deal. If all the extras or problems are brought out at the beginning, it's so easy for the landlord to just say "No!" He's got nothing invested in you. You don't conform to his requirements. "No!" is the easiest thing to say.

On the other hand, after three days of negotiating (all that time spent looking at the rental and thinking about it was negotiating, whether either of you realized it or not), it's a different story. Now the landlord has a vested interest in finding a way to make it work. He wants you, so he'll paint. In the end, he really can't abide the pets. So he increases the deposit to make it work. If he had not spent time getting to know you, the answer to both would surely have been, "No."

TIP

The more time invested in a deal, the more each party has to lose if it doesn't go through. Any time spent considering the deal always increases the chances of getting the other party to say, "Yes!"

Of course, this applies to all types of real estate transactions, not just rentals. I've sat with sellers/buyers into the wee hours of the night while they tried to decide whether or not to accept a particular condition (such as the interest rate on a mortgage, the date of occupancy, or even the price) of a sales offer. They might not like the condition, they might not want the condition, they might be inclined to refuse it. But after having spent six hours or more discussing it, the thought of simply giving up without getting some kind of deal becomes abhorrent. In some cases, it actually becomes a challenge to try to figure out how to make it work. Thus, the sellers/buyers no longer simply wrestle with whether or not they want the particular condition in question, but instead worry over accepting that condition or losing everything. The fact that there's something to lose is a result of investing not money, but time.

TRAP

Until you've got just what you want, don't hurry the negotiations. The more time you get the other party to spend considering the deal, the more likely he or she is to accept your offer, regardless of what it is.

Set a Deadline

If you've ever watched a telethon fund raiser, you quickly realize that 90 percent of the money is raised in the last hour. That's regardless of how long the telethon lasts, whether it's 5 hours or 50. It isn't until it gets down to the actual deadline that people contribute.

It's the same in journalism. Talk to any reporter and he or she will tell you that both their bane and their salvation is the deadline. They hate deadlines because of the pressure, yet they would never get a story written without them. (It also applies to writing books, as the publisher of this one will quickly tell you!)

TIP

No deal ever closes without a deadline.

The same is true in real estate. This is not to discount the element of invested time that was noted above, but deadlines are also crucial. (By the way, deadlines and "time invested" are not contradictions, but two sides of the same coin. Yes, you are far more likely to get what you want if you get the other party to invest time. But you'll never get what you want until the deal closes and, in most cases, it won't close without a deadline.)

The best example of this is in the sales offer that a buyer makes to a seller. All sales agreements give the buyer the opportunity to state just how long the offer will be open.

Usually this deadline is the last consideration of the buyer. Time is always of the essence in any deal, and while it is possible to make an open-ended offer, "until accepted" (most unwise as we shall see) most offers give the seller a specified time within which to accept.

I have sat in with sales agents who advised their buyer clients, "Give the seller a week to think it over. She might go along with your deal." That's a lot of hooey! In a week, the seller may receive three other offers, two better than yours. Further, in a week the seller may have talked herself into your offer—and then out of it.

The best advice, in my opinion, is to set a deadline that forces the seller to come up with a decision. In most cases, that's just one day, 24 hours, or less.

I can hear the protests from those real estate agents who strongly believe in giving the other party plenty of time. But I stick to my guns. Setting a deadline, a realistic deadline, is the best way of getting your offer accepted. Here's why:

- *It's Enough Time.* Assuming that the sellers can be reached, one day usually gives them plenty of time to consider the offer. If they begin looking at it by six o'clock, they should fully understand it by seven, and they can chew it over by ten o'clock. That's enough time for them to invest so that they will feel that if they simply reject it, they will have lost something (time invested).

- *Sellers Seldom Accept First Offers.* The theme of this book, after all, is negotiation, and sellers often see the initial offer for what it probably is: a "trial balloon," the first step in negotiations. While it's true that a seller who counters the offer has legally rejected it and given the buyer complete freedom to walk away from the deal, most sellers are willing to take that chance. They understand that often the buyer is actually looking for some sort of counteroffer with which to work. In other words, the process of buying a property usually involves offer, counteroffer, counter-counteroffer, and so on. Thus, one way to get to the counteroffer is to set a deadline.

- *Procrastination Is Easier Than Action.* Consider it from the seller's (or other party's) perspective. They've received an offer. It's not what they want. The price is off; the terms are wrong. What are they to do?

If there's no deadline, one appealing thing to do is nothing. If they don't act, maybe the buyer will have a change of heart and sweeten the offer. Further, if they wait, maybe some other person will come in with a better offer. Putting off making a decision, without a deadline, can often be the most tempting decision.

On the other hand, if there is a deadline, some action is forced. If no action is taken, the deal is dead. The only way to keep it alive is with action. (In real estate, if an offer is not accepted by the deadline, it's automatically dead.) When there's a deadline, procrastinating threatens the loss of the deal. It now becomes preferable to take action.

From the buyer's perspective, setting a deadline may be the best way to get the seller to act. Either the seller will outright accept the offer, reject the offer, or make a counteroffer. In my experience, most often the counteroffer is the result. Once the counteroffer (with its own deadline for the buyer) is made, the negotiations can move forward. Keep in mind that as counteroffers are made, both parties are investing increasing amounts of time in the deal. (See Chapter 12 for more information on working with an agent and deadlines.)

TRAP

Just because you set deadlines doesn't mean you'll always get the deal you want. The deadline should be considered one tool to be used in conjunction with many others. Beware of turning a deadline into a "take it or leave it" threat. As we'll see shortly, this works less often than most people think.

Act in a Timely Fashion

Once again, we're not in contradiction to the rule about investing time. Yes, you want the other party to invest time. But you don't want to lose out to a better offer from someone else.

I can remember a broker friend working with buyers a few years ago, a very nice young couple, who wanted a home in a suburban area near San Francisco. Their problem, however, was that the Bay Area is very expensive, one of the most expensive in the United States. Homes in the neighborhood in which they were looking started at about $800,000 in price and went up from there. The most they could afford to pay, however, given the loan they could get and the down payment they had, was $775,000. They were, in effect, out of the market. But, they were determined, and they felt, correctly, that over time a desperate seller or two might pop up who would sell at a lower price.

It took several months, but the broker did find some sellers who wanted to get out immediately and were willing to accept a lower price to accomplish that. The sellers had already purchased another property; it was at the end of December, the worst season for selling a home; and they knew they had to compromise. They were asking $825,000, which was over market, but indicated they would probably settle for $775,000, just inside the buyers' range.

The trouble was that the buyers were finicky. They weren't sure about the room arrangement of the house, the size of the kitchen seemed small, and the wife simply couldn't abide the fact that there was no fireplace in the master bedroom. The broker agreed that these were, indeed, all problems with the property, but that because of their financial situation they had to compromise to get in. Further, sellers willing to sell for a low price were few and far between, and unless the buyers acted quickly, they could lose out.

But the buyers weren't sure. They saw the house on Sunday, again the next Wednesday, and yet again the following weekend. But they couldn't make up their minds about making an offer. Finally, two weeks later, they had talked it out and decided they could live with the property. They called the broker to say they would make a $775,000 offer. The broker, sadly, informed them that other buyers had offered the same amount and the seller had already sold.

Needless to say, these buyers were unhappy and resolved to act more quickly in the future. Unfortunately, spring was coming, there were more buyers in the market, and they never did find another lower-priced house in that neighborhood.

TIP

Strike while the iron's hot. Real estate is a highly competitive field in all aspects. If you don't act quickly, someone else will, and you could lose out on the deal.

Negotiating a deal can only take place when there are two parties. If you wait too long, the other party may already have negotiated a deal with someone else.

As a practical matter, when buying a home, jump in with both feet and learn everything about the market as fast as you can. Go out with brokers, visit homes for sale, check with Realty Boards, and familiarize yourself with what's out there and with what homes should cost. That way, you'll recognize what you want when you see it and be able to act quickly. Remember, in a hot market where multiple offers are often made, you may have to act after seeing the property for only a few moments. Of course, in a slow market, you may have days or even weeks to act, but even then procrastination can let someone else sneak in and steal your deal.

The Bottom Line

These, then, are the three areas where you can control time, or be controlled by it:

Investing in time

Setting a deadline

Acting in a timely fashion

3
Play the Players

The basis for this chapter comes from an old friend of mine named Harry, who was a great poker player. In the past, Harry and I would go to a game, and after an evening of playing, I'd look down and be happy because I'd won 50 bucks. When I'd go over to see Harry, he was often ahead 500 bucks.

When I asked Harry his secret for winning at cards, he replied, "I don't play the cards . . . I play the people."

Well, he certainly knew his cards, but he knew the other players even better. He could "tell" when another player was bluffing or held a higher hand. And he knew when he held the winning cards.

Negotiating real estate is much like playing poker. Yes, you certainly have to know how the mechanics of a deal work. But, almost more important, you have to know how to play the people you're dealing with. You will always be working with people. Deals don't exist in a vacuum; deals are about people. But how you handle the people with whom you deal often determines how successful you are at negotiating. I believe that the people-part of any deal is the most important.

Never Offend the Buyer/Seller

It's often been said that in real estate the three most important words in determining price are, "Location, location, location!"

When negotiating, the three most important words are, "Don't get personal!"

I've seen this rule violated more times than I want to remember. Typically it occurs in a purchase. A buyer wants a home and offers what she thinks is a reasonable price. The seller, however, figures it's worth a lot more and is offended by the offer, so he turns it down and counters at only slightly less than the asking price. Now the buyer has been put in a huff by the intransigent seller. So long as buyer and seller do not personally meet, but negotiations are carried out through a broker (something I do not always recommend, as we'll see shortly), progress on the deal can continue.

But just let the typical buyer and seller meet for five minutes and the deal is history. The buyer will quickly tell the seller how ridiculous the counteroffer is. The seller will tell the buyer that she can't recognize true value. The buyer may counter with a comment about the seller's deficient intelligence. The seller may make a disparaging remark about the buyer's forebears. Negotiations very quickly break down into dispute. Both sides take umbrage and neither wants to deal with the other "no matter what the price!"

Of course, in the real world no one is going to refuse to buy or sell "no matter the price." But if the buyer offends the seller (or vice versa), the price could end up being a lot worse for the offending party.

TIP

 When you're negotiating, think of it as business. Yes, occasionally you may want to appear injured or aggrieved by something the other party says or does, but only as a ploy. Never take it personally, and if you're smart, never do anything to let the other side take it personally. You don't want to be put in the position of having to apologize to save the deal.

The wisdom of never offending the other party came home to me when a close friend was involved in a quarrel over a purchase. My friend had bought a bare lot in the mountains and began construction on a home. During excavation for the foundation, she discovered an old, large, unused diesel storage tank was buried there. It had been used to store fuel for logging equipment. The contractors began removing the tank only to discover it still contained some fuel and was leaking. The ground surrounding it was soaked in diesel fuel. The building inspector noticed this and eventually the county environmentalist required that hundreds of yards of contaminated soil be hauled 350 miles away to a toxic-waste dumpsite. The cost was more than $10,000 and my friend, naturally, wanted the seller to pay for it.

The seller "stonewalled" and claimed that he had disclosed the problem and that my buyer friend had understood and agreed to shoulder all the cost of removal. That, in fact, was the reason he had sold for what he claimed was such a low price.

According to my friend, this was simply untrue and she had every right to be offended. Her legal recourse was to get an attorney and sue. At the very least, the seller would have had to pay some of the cost—very likely all of it.

But my friend really didn't want to expend the time, emotional stress, and cost of litigation (something more people should consider before going to court). So she negotiated instead. She met with the seller and she did indeed bring her attorney, who in no uncertain terms explained what he could and fully intended to do to the seller.

However, my friend was cordial, never mentioned the obvious (that the seller had outright lied and was continuing to lie), chatted in a friendly matter, and made it perfectly clear that she didn't consider this a personal matter. It was strictly business.

The next day, the seller called my buyer friend on the phone and asked if there wasn't some way they could compromise. She replied that it was nice of him to call, but she really didn't see how a compromise was possible. He had put the tank in. Between the two of them, they both knew she hadn't known about it. However, if he wanted to pay for removal costs, she would certainly not add on any of the hefty legal charges that were sure to be involved in a lawsuit. He said he would think it over.

Two days later he called back and said that because she was such "a nice gal," he'd take care of it.

Yes, it's obvious he was wrong, she was right, and it ended the way it should. But consider what the outcome could have been if my friend had taken it personally, accused the seller of lying, refused to talk to him, or even attacked him personally. He may have felt cornered and

forced to hire his own attorney to defend himself. The ultimate outcome might have been similar, but it could have taken years, cost tens
of thousands of dollars for each of them, and kept my friend from getting on with her life.

TRAP

Beware of taking your frustrations out on the other
party. You may just give them the ammunition they
need to shoot you down.

Think about it. Would you rather deal with someone whom you find
pleasant and likeable or with someone whose guts you hate? Would
you prefer to pick up the phone and call a person who you know will
respond warmly, or someone who will start yelling at you? Years ago I
had a boundary dispute with a landowner and called him to ask if we
couldn't find a way to work together and settle it. He harangued me
on the phone, accused me of trying to pressure him (which I was not
doing), called me a liar and a cheat, and finished by telling me he'd
"see me in court." Now, was I going to call him back and attempt to
work out an amicable settlement? Or was I going to wash my hands of
it and turn it over to my attorney to handle? In the end, I did prevail.
But it took longer, cost more, and to this day we still don't speak
though we own property next door to each other.

Beware of Choosing "Nice" People to Represent You

This is a simple rule to understand, but difficult to follow. Most buyers and sellers of real estate are average people who really don't
want a lot of hassle in their lives. Therefore, when it comes time to
find an agent, they often choose the "nicest" one. That usually
means the agent who is pleasant, offers them the least amount of
resistance or trouble, goes along with what they say, and generally
makes them feel good.

But, that's not necessarily the best agent to have. For example,
when selling a property, it's the agent's duty to inform the seller of

the true market price of the property, as best they can calculate it. But sellers often don't like to hear that their property is worth less than they think it is. So the "nice" agent may just agree with whatever price the sellers have in mind, hoping that later on, when it doesn't sell, they'll come down. The sellers would be better off with a hard-nosed agent who would say, "You may want $330,000, but it's only worth $315,000." That's not a nice thing to say. But if it's the truth, it may mean the difference between selling or waiting and not being able to dump the property immediately.

I've seen buyers who fall in love with an agent who takes them all around showing them wonderful properties, most of which they can't afford. Or an agent who doesn't inform a buyer that an offer he or she is making is unrealistically low. (It's the agent's duty to inform a buyer if the offer is unlikely to be accepted, not argue with the buyer and try to coerce him or her to raise it.) Or, in the worst case, an agent who is so nice that he or she writes up a buyer's offer with the price and all the conditions they want. Then, when the sellers reject it out of hand, takes back a counteroffer with the price and all the conditions the sellers want, never making any effort to be realistic with either buyer or seller. The result, almost always, is no deal. The agent is simply too "nice" to be a good negotiator.

TIP

I want an agent who represents me to be hard-nosed, irritating, and determined; to have learned his or her business in the backrooms; and to tell it like it is and get what he or she goes after. I want the other guy to have the "nice" agent.

Only Deal with the Person Who Has the Power to Decide

Would you walk onto a car lot and try to buy an automobile from the person who's standing there washing the cars? Would you go into a jewelry store and attempt to buy a gold ring from a security guard? Would you try to buy stock from a broker's receptionist or place a classified ad with the newspaper delivery boy?

These examples of dealing with the wrong person are obvious, yet every day in real estate people do attempt to deal with people who don't have the power to decide, who don't have any more power to conclude a deal than a car washer, security guard, receptionist, or delivery boy.

For example, you own a duplex that you want to rent and you spend several hours talking to a fellow who seems very interested, only to learn that, in his family, the decision to rent is made solely by his wife. Or you're a seller who's trying to sell "by owner" and you spend half a day trying to convince a person to buy, only to realize later that the person is a real estate agent who isn't interested in buying and only wants to list. (Agents are ethically bound to reveal their professional status to you immediately, but . . .) Or you're a buyer who wants to secure financing and you spend a morning with a mortgage broker only to find out that he doesn't represent any lenders who will give you a loan given your financial condition (although other lenders might).

The problem here is simply one of dealing with the wrong person. Get to the right person and you'll be able to sew up a deal quickly. But if you're working with the spouse who doesn't make the decisions, the agent instead of the principal, or the representative instead of directly with the lender, you could be wasting your time, getting frustrated, and, potentially, lose out on a good deal.

Go Directly to the Buyer/Seller

I want to introduce a theme that will recur throughout this book, namely that if you're a good negotiator, you may want to change the normal system of handling a real estate negotiation. Normally, the buyer/seller uses the real estate agent as the negotiator or intermediary. I'm suggesting that you may want to negotiate directly—yourself.

Before those old-time real estate agents who know the value of the broker/principal relationship begin to thrash me, let me qualify the above statement. I have long maintained that the average person was far better off letting the real estate agent handle negotiations than trying it by himself or herself. That's because the average person is not skilled at negotiation. Discussing a deal can quickly degenerate into a confrontation, people can take things personally, knock heads together, and the deal can go out the window.

However, the assumption that the buyer or the seller or both are not skilled negotiators and the real estate agent is likewise is not always true.

If you are a skilled negotiator, you should consider negotiating directly with the seller. See Chapter 12 for more information on this topic.

Always Strive for the Moral High Ground

This may seem to be a peculiar rule since, after all, you're presumably not trying to do anything dishonest or illegal. However, there are more ways to kill a deal than being dishonest or illegal. If you portray yourself as tricky, underhanded, or sneaky you are sure to undermine the other side's confidence in you, and once that's eroded, successful negotiating will become increasingly difficult.

For example, I once had a buyer (I represented the seller) who presented an earnest money check for $2,500. I noticed that he had written out "fifteen hundred" while using the numbers, "2,500." For all practical purposes the check was uncashable and useless. Of course, it could simply have been an accident in writing out the check, which is what he claimed, and he eventually wrote out a new and correct draft. However, my seller was put on guard and thereafter saw the buyer as sneaky and untrustworthy. Negotiations became awkward because, from that point on, the seller trusted nothing the buyer said or did. Eventually, the sale fell through, I believe simply because the buyer tried to pull a fast one on the deposit check.

In another instance, the seller described the property as being in perfect condition with no faults or problems. But an inspection revealed a drainage problem that caused the basement area to flood each winter. There was no way the seller could not have known about this, and from that time forth, the buyer was suspicious about everything in the house, demanded a second inspection, and challenged all sorts of things from the roof not leaking to there being proper wiring. Eventually the deal was made, but only after extended negotiations, written inspection reports, and concessions on the part of the seller with regard to price and financing. All of this could have been avoided if the seller had simply come clean right at the beginning.

TIP

Successful negotiations are built on trust. Anything you do to limit or destroy that trust will harm those negotiations.

This has some subtler ramifications as well. Let's say that there is some matter over which you refuse to compromise. Maybe the buyer wants you to rebuild a wall at the back of the property that is currently leaning over and looking as if it might fall. You don't want to rebuild, and you simply say, "No."

Now the buyer begins thinking to herself, "Why doesn't he want to do that? Is it just the money? Or is there something about that wall that he's not revealing? Maybe the ground out there is bad. Maybe there's a problem with the neighbor. Maybe . . ."

An arbitrary refusal to yield on your part can be interpreted as an ethical problem—you have something to hide. On the other hand, if you refuse to yield, but provide an explanation that is reasonable, your motives are no longer suspect. For example, you explain you had that wall fixed just two years ago. You paid a lot of money and the workers simply did a bad job. As a matter of principle, you simply will not pay for it again.

"Okay," the buyer may think. "You're not too smart when it comes to hiring a wall contractor. You're stubborn about taking a loss. I can live with that, so long as you're not trying to cheat me!" Your explanation makes it rational and understandable. You're still operating on a high moral plane.

TIP

Never do anything that will make you look like a sneaky person. Always portray yourself as taking the moral high ground. You are making a legitimate offer with a legitimate deposit check. You are willing to make any legitimate compromise. It makes you look reasonable and trustworthy. It gives your opponents the hope that you're someone with whom they can, and will want to, deal.

TRAP

It's almost impossible to make a deal with someone who is, or at least appears to be, untrustworthy. If the other side is so distrustful that the only way they'll deal is through their lawyer, you can probably kiss the sale goodbye. Most deals are actually made on a handshake (trust) with the paperwork to follow.

The Bottom Line

The rules for working with people are:

Never offend the buyer/seller.

Beware of choosing "nice" people to represent you.

Only deal with a person who has the power to decide.

Go directly to the buyer/seller.

Never believe anyone else is entirely on your side.

Always strive for the moral high ground.

4
Learn to Act

I once had an actor friend who, though not particularly famous, was indeed a good actor. I can still remember an occasion when I was waiting for him outside a restaurant where we were planning to have lunch. I scanned the street in both directions, looking at the people passing by, expecting him to show up but not seeing him.

Suddenly, he said, "Hello, Bob," and he was standing right next to me. I jumped. How had he gotten there without my seeing him approach? Then I realized that I had been looking for a man in a flannel shirt (my friend always wore flannel shirts) with a big stride. I had seen the man next to me wearing a dark jacket and stumbling up to me with a lame leg. But I hadn't given him a second glance because he wasn't what I was looking for. Rather, I had in my mind an image of my friend and I was trying to apply it to everyone on the street.

In computer technology terms, my *image recognition software* was at fault. As a practical matter, simply by wearing an unexpected dark-colored jacket and by limping a little, my friend had completely disguised himself to me. Of course, he was simply doing it as an exercise, a part of his trade. Nevertheless, it brought home to me the point that people aren't always who they seem. Indeed, sometimes people can purposely be different from who they are. And that can lead to certain negotiating advantages—or if you're unprepared, disadvantages.

Disarm a Psychological Attack by Drawing Attention to It

Thus far we've been discussing strategies that will help you to get what you want when negotiating. In essence, we've been fighting fair. Everything is aboveboard and out in the open.

However, sometimes you'll get into a negotiation that's dirty. The other side may not play by the rules of good conduct. The other side may resort to psychological warfare.

You're a woman and you're presenting an offer to buy a property to a male seller. He is very nice to you. He pulls out the chair for you to sit down. He asks if you'd like some coffee or other refreshment. It's nice, but a bit irritating. There are two agents present and he begins addressing them and ignoring you, even though you're the principal, the buyer. You hear remarks such as, "She probably can't understand this, so let's see if we can make it simpler," or "Let the lady talk before we get on with things,"" or, after you make a comment, "She's sweet, isn't she?"

Yes, the remarks are obviously sexist. But more important to the deal, they are condescending. Their real intent is to neutralize you as a force, a power in the negotiations. They aim to reduce the value of your opinions and arguments. If you let them continue, you won't be able to participate as an equal member and will ultimately get a much lesser deal.

This is a psychological attack on you. The way to counter it is to bring it out in the open. You might say something such as, "I can't help but notice that many of your remarks are disparaging toward my gender. If you're hoping to get a better deal by belittling me, I'm afraid you're wasting your time. I'm the buyer and you have to deal directly with me."

I don't think you'll hear many more condescending remarks.

Or, let's say you're a seller whose property has gone up in value enormously since you bought it 20 years ago. Just by chance, the area turned into one of the most desirable neighborhoods in the state.) You paid $25,000. Today, it's selling for $970,000. Of course, that's a lot of money to you since your income has never been over $35,000 a year.

You're starting to negotiate with the buyer's agent, who smiles at you and says, "It's amazing isn't it. You're going to get nearly a million dollars for your property. Isn't it wonderful?"

Of course it's wonderful, and you smile back. Then he continues, "I know you don't know about big money. This is sort of out of your league, isn't it? Why don't you sit back and let me handle things?"

Again, this is a psychological attack. If it happens once, you can ignore it and just figure the other party is a jerk. If it continues to occur and begins to affect your ability to negotiate, you can end it by bringing attention to it.

"You seem to be suggesting that because this deal involves a large sum of money, I'm somehow less capable. I consider this a friendly, though rather obvious, attempt to gain a psychological advantage. I assure you I am not going to settle for less just because of the amounts involved." Having said that, there's every chance you will get every penny you deserve.

Psychological attacks usually are intended to belittle you in one way or another. As we've seen, they might be aimed at your gender or background. They could just as easily be targeted at your intelligence or your experience. For example, as a buyer you insist on presenting your own offer. You sit down to negotiate and the seller's agent immediately asks, "Are you a real estate broker?"

"No," you reply truthfully.

"Are you at least a real estate salesperson?"

Again, "No."

You hear a "Humph." You shrug and begin presenting your offer. As you are doing so you hear, "Someone who had experience in real estate would never make an offer like this." Later, "The terminology is all wrong; we'll have to rewrite it." Then, perhaps a little more directly, "Wouldn't you feel more comfortable having an agent or someone who knows what they're doing present this?"

Please keep in mind that it doesn't matter whether your offer is good or bad or whether you know what you're doing or not. You are being psychologically attacked at the level of your experience and knowledge. The other party isn't saying, "I don't like your offer," or "I want to negotiate some of the terms or the price." He or she is saying, "You're too naive or too stupid to be in this game." The attack is personal, and if you let it continue, you may soon feel embarrassed and may find yourself accepting terms, conditions, and a price that you don't want.

Again, the way to disarm this attack is to bring it out in the open. "Am I hearing correctly? Are you saying that I'm too ignorant to make an offer on your property? I'm the first to acknowledge that I don't know it all, but I'm ready and able to learn. If there's a problem with my offer, something you don't understand or that you find is presented in an unclear manner, tell me what it is and I'll explain it further. In the future, however, I suggest we stick with the issues and avoid personal attacks."

TRAP

If you allow the other party to continue a psychological attack unhindered, he or she may press it to the point where you will lose in a deal.

TIP

As soon as you unveil a psychological attack for what it is, its power vanishes and the other side will be forced to stop using it.

The real trick, of course, is to avoid succumbing to the psychological attack. If you believe that you are weaker because of your gender, or that you don't know how to handle "serious money," or that you're stupid or ignorant, then you lose automatically. On the other hand, if you've a bit of self-confidence and recognize the attack for what it is—nothing more than a weapon (albeit a dirty one) in negotiations—you can neutralize it by bringing it out into the open.

I've had some small experience with computers and am occasionally called upon to help teach people the rudiments of how to use them. Very often these people are totally computer illiterate, and worse, having never worked with a computer, they are very intimidated by them.

I have learned that the first thing I must do is get rid of their intimidation, or else they'll never learn anything about computers. So I always tell them, "If you think you can't learn to use a computer, you never will. On the other hand, if you believe you can learn to use one, I can have you up and running in 30 minutes."

In negotiating real estate it would go something like this. "If you believe the psychological attack the other party makes, you'll never get the deal you want. But if you believe that it's just a weapon used by the other side and disarm it by bringing it to everyone's attention, you've got a good chance of getting everything you want."

Be Irrational, Occasionally

TIP

If the seller thinks you're a little bit crazy, he or she may be more inclined to accept a goofy offer. After all, what can you expect from someone who's nuts?

This doesn't mean you should be carrying on conversations with spirits or foaming at the mouth. Rather, it means that you always want to keep the other side guessing about what you will and won't do. One of the best ways to accomplish this is to make them think you're a little bit *irrational*. (The word, after all, suggests that you take actions that to others appear to be against your own advantage. In truth it really means that others simply don't understand your "rationale.") There's nothing better to help you to keep your morale high than to know you have the other side off balance.

The best application of this rule that I ever saw had nothing to do with real estate. Instead it was in the world of politics. President Richard Nixon always sought to keep his opponents off balance by convincing them that he was just a tiny bit crazy. Push him too far, and who knows what could happen? As President he might launch nuclear missiles . . . or send troops into Cambodia . . . or reconcile differences with China. He even said as much.

While it remains for history ultimately to judge his actions, to me it seems clear that Nixon, in truth, may have been many things, but was anything but irrational. I can still remember his fall from popularity during the scandal over the break-in at the Democratic headquarters in the Watergate building. Nixon was vilified and Congressional hearings were held to minutely investigate every aspect of his presidency, including audio tapes of conversations. He was put under a microscopic examination that very few of us could have survived emotionally. Newspaper and television pundits repeatedly wondered about his grasp on reality and his ability to handle presidential issues given the stress of the situation. People feared the "irrationality factor." And that gave him an edge. Nobody wanted to push him too far. In my opinion, it allowed him to hang on for far longer than he might otherwise have been able to.

Yet, from his perspective, it seems to me he acted with great rationality through it all. While under fire, he continued to fulfill the basic functions of his office as best he could, given the circumstances. Only when it became "perfectly clear" that he had completely lost the support of his own party did he choose to resign. And he did that with remarkable grace.

The man was certainly calculating. But I seriously doubt if anything he ever did could be considered truly irrational.

Something similar (in terms of "acting" irrational) was the case with a friend I once had. Jerry bought and sold an enormous amount of investment real estate, making quite a bit of profit along the way. He negotiated his own deals with buyers or sellers, although I occasionally sat in as an agent. Often, just when things were the most serious in the negotiations, he would surreptitiously wink at me and all hell would break loose. Once, I had trouble concealing a smile when, in the middle of a serious discussion about price, Jerry asked a seller if he would accept a truckload of potatoes to sweeten the deal.

The poor seller didn't know if my friend was making a real offer or was just plain crazy. And Jerry didn't help him out. He began extolling the virtues of baked potatoes, fried potatoes, even potato skins. He said he could have them delivered and dumped at the seller's back door.

"I don't want potatoes," the seller said in frustration. "I just want to work this deal."

"It's potatoes or nothing," Jerry replied, and went into the kitchen for a cup of coffee.

The seller leaned over and asked if Jerry had a problem. I replied that he was a serious buyer making a serious offer, although he himself was a bit eccentric. The seller nodded agreement. Later that evening the seller accepted Jerry's offer almost in total.

Why would irrationality help Jerry? When my friend pulled one of his calculated "irrationality" stunts, more often than not the routine broke the carefully built up understanding of my friend the other party had. One moment the other person, buyer or seller, thought he or she had a handle on what Jerry really wanted out of the deal and how far he could be bent. The next, the other party was thrown into confusion, concluding that he or she really had no idea what Jerry's bottom line really was.

Of course, it doesn't always work that well. Sometimes, when you're dealing with a really solid adversary, it doesn't work at all. But, as with other devices, it can cause a "change up," which acts to keep your opponent off balance.

Strive to Be Innocent

Have you ever noticed that as soon as someone admits they really don't understand something, a lot of people rush in to help him or her out? Try it with a group of friends. The subject doesn't really matter, but wait until real estate comes up and then say something like, "I hate to admit it, but a lease/option is over my head. What exactly is it?"

You've just given all the people around you who know (or think they know) what a lease/option is the opportunity to shine. They can suddenly show off their knowledge and be "good guys" at the same time by helping you out. It's hard to turn down such an appealing role. Of course, now you listen and learn what they know . . . and don't know. Appearing innocent is a great way to learn a lot.

I have a friend in real estate, Chet, who is both a broker and an investor. When it comes time to negotiate, he kind of turns the toe of one foot inward, looks a little shy, and in the best country boy fashion says something like, "Shucks, I'm just the new guy here. You people are all the experts, so you're going to have to help me out understanding this deal."

The others usually smile to each other thinking that they have this pigeon just where they want him. Then they take Chet under their wings to "help him out." Of course, that's usually just when Chet has them where he wants them. In the course of their explaining the deal to Chet, the others often reveal much more than they'd care to about their own needs and what they'd be willing to concede.

After a while, Chet knows a whole lot more about them and what they want, must have, and can afford to give away than they do about him. In fact, they usually know nothing at all about him or his thinking. So when he kind of smiles self-consciously and says with humility, "Shucks, I don't really know if this is a fair offer, so you tell me because you know a whole lot more about these things than I do, but why don't you give up this . . . and this . . . , which you just said you don't care about, and take this . . . and this . . . , which you just said you want, and maybe then we can all shake hands and go home?" They are often taken completely by surprise.

TIP

Watch out for anyone who starts out by saying, "Shucks!" There is no real meaning for this word! It's just a cover for establishing the role of an innocent. And in real estate negotiations there are very few innocents left.

Sarah was a real estate investor with more than 30 years of solid experience. Yet she never came into negotiations bragging about her knowledge. In fact, she tried to conceal it in a most unusual way. She would feign deafness in one ear.

Have you ever noticed what happens when someone deaf is trying to hear what's being said? Everyone around suddenly speaks not only louder and slower, but also in easier to understand terms. Yet the deaf person is only hard of hearing, not stupid.

Once I was present when Sarah was negotiating to buy a duplex. She had been presented as a tough negotiator and the seller was obviously worried about how big a price concession he would have to make.

Sarah simply came in, shook hands, and presented an offer for $325,000. The seller had been asking $357,000. It was a significant $27,000 price reduction.

The seller put up a good show and said, "My price is $357,000."

But every time the seller told her his price, she would lean forward and say, "What?" The seller would repeat the price, only somehow each time it was just a little bit lower.

"What?"

"I said my price was $357,000," the seller repeated, "but I am willing to drop it down to $355,000 to make the deal."

"What?"

"$355,000, I said I was willing to take $355,000. Of course, I suppose I could go lower."

"What?"

"I said I could go lower, maybe $354,000?"

"What?"

"Oh, all right. My bottom price is $330,000. I can't afford to go any lower than that."

"What?"

The seller picked up the offer, looked at the $325,000 bid, shook his head, and simply signed.

I always wondered just how low that seller might have gone if Sarah had continued to "What?" her way through the negotiations.

TRAP

Most of us are too eager to show off just how much we know. This can work against us. For example, what if the other party says that since we're acting the expert we should tell them how to proceed? If we jump into the breach, we can often reveal too much too soon about what we're willing to give up to get the deal. Let go of the ego-satisfying position of know-it-all and instead assume the profit-making position of innocent.

TIP

Ask the people on the other side for their advice. Invite their criticism. Be willing to have them analyze your offer. This will only make you look humble and in need of help. Say something such as, "This is what I want. But, perhaps I don't fully understand. Maybe there's something about this deal that needs to be explained. Could you please enlighten me?" In their rush to criticize, advise, and analyze, they will trip over themselves revealing what it is they really want and how far they are willing to go to get it. All that it costs to learn about your opponents is a little humility.

Always Ask "Why?"

Sometimes seemingly impossible demands will threaten to shut down a deal. For example, you're a buyer and the seller keeps insisting that you be ready to fund your new mortgage within 14 days. You've already contacted a mortgage broker and know that it's going to take a month or more, given the volume of loans being processed at that time. You say you need longer, but the seller keeps hitting you over the head with that two-week limitation. No, he won't give you more time. The demand is sucking the energy right out of the deal.

To keep things alive, you may say you'll try to get funded in two weeks, even though you know full well it's impossible. You're hoping that after the time is up, the seller will give you some more time.

Instead, you could simply ask the seller, "Why are you insisting on 14 days?"

"Why?" is often the biggest single weapon in a negotiation. Yet many people are simply afraid to ask. I suspect they don't want to know the answer for fear it will ruin the deal entirely. Maybe there's an absolutely immutable reason the seller must have 14 days. And as soon as you hear it, you'll know the deal is blown away. But isn't it better to know up front where you stand than to wait two weeks to find out? Besides, there are very few absolutely immutable reasons.

The seller may say, "I've got a backup offer and if you don't qualify, I'll take it." Now, at least, you know what you've got to deal with. Asking why has revealed the problem and maybe there's a solution. Perhaps you could show the seller your credit report and credit score as well as a preapproval letter from the lender saying you are well qualified. Yes, your deal will go through, but you need four weeks instead of two. Maybe you could increase the deposit as assurance of your confidence?

The point is, if you don't ask, "Why?" you won't find out. If you do, chances are you'll learn useful information.

Let's consider a different example. The buyer insists on a price lower than market, even though as a seller you've already offered to sell for what recent comparables have gone for. Instead of continuing to argue, you simply ask, "Why do you really insist on such a low price?"

Again, you might not like the answer. Perhaps the buyer will say, "My brother bought a house for that price in this neighborhood two years ago. I'm not paying more."

You might point out that two years ago the area was in recession. Today it's recovering and prices are higher. But chances are that this buyer is determined not to be "bettered" by his sibling and won't budge. Now it really is a brick wall you're up against.

However, a person who finds price all important is often more than willing to dicker on the terms. You might ask the buyer to give you a second mortgage at an interest rate well above market. If he does that, maybe it's worth your while to give him his price. You get terms that make a lower price worthwhile to you. Of course, it never would happen unless you asked, "Why?"

One problem with the "Why?" question is that as negotiations get tougher, the other party is less and less inclined to be forthright in answering. When asked, "Why?" in the middle to the end of a negotiation, many people are immediately suspicious of the question and the questioner. Is the other party trying to learn information that will give him or her an edge? Why should I tell them anything that might give them ammunition for getting a better deal?

Trust is now all important. If you established trust early on, if you've stuck to the moral high road, you probably will get a straight answer. If not, asking "Why?" in the middle to the end of negotiations might produce a guarded answer.

TIP

Most people are afraid to reveal their true motivations. Asking "Why?" may get them out into the open. However, many times it is a mistake to conceal your true motivations. If the other side knows what you truly want, they may be able to give it to you.

TRAP

Sometimes you do want to keep your motivations to yourself. Maybe you've learned that a new commercial center is going in next to a store you want to buy and it will double the store's value. To reveal your motivation will cause the seller to refuse the deal or to increase the price.

Question Authority

"Question authority" is an old phrase out of the 1960s when the flower children believed that everyone over 30 was the enemy. Of course, all of the flower children are now over 60, so I suppose it no longer applies in a sociological setting. But it does have a special meaning in real estate.

When you're negotiating, the other side may sometimes take all the energy out of a deal with their "authority." If you let them continue, they could kill the deal.

For example, I was involved in the sale of a home near the coastline. The buyer's agent kept insisting that the seller should lower the price because the house was run down and small and the Coastal Commission would prevent any buyer from improving the property. The seller wasn't going to lower the price, and I could see the life slipping out of the deal. I had to reenergize it.

I wasn't that familiar with the Coastal Commission regulations, but I did know they were very strict when it came to anyone building within their jurisdiction. But, I suspected, not as strict as the buyer's agent portrayed. So I challenged her, saying I didn't think the buyer would be precluded from improving anything on the inside of the property and probably could add on to the outside, but with a permit.

She immediately said I was wrong, that I didn't know the rules (which technically was true), and that she did because she handled properties in this area all the time. Now there was a decision to be made. The seller and I could either accept her as the authority or we could challenge further. We decided to take it another step. I halted the negotiations and called the Commission on my cell phone. I was referred to a local attorney who handled a lot of cases involving their rulings. By contacting the attorney we discovered that yes indeed they were strict, but the kind of changes that this buyer wanted to make would probably be allowed without much difficulty. Suddenly the buyer's agent's arguments for a lower price disappeared . . . and the seller got a better deal.

When it's the authority that's causing you a problem in a deal, challenge it. Usually the worst you can do is discover that the authority is right. But often the best you can do is to find out that the authority is wrong.

On the other hand, sometimes the authority is only an opinion. For example, you may be involved in a transaction where the critical factor is whether or not you, the buyer, will qualify for a particular mortgage. If you qualify, the deal will go through because both parties are agreed on price and other terms. But if you don't qualify, then there's no deal. You have a preapproval letter, but it was issued a week earlier for a different property you originally wanted and is for a smaller amount than needed.

The seller's agent, on the spot and hoping to bring in her own offer, may say your preapproval letter proves you won't qualify for the deal. The seller looks at you and you see that the deal's history, *unless* you can counter the "authority." So you call up the original mortgage broker (assuming you're the buyer), hopefully one with whom you've already made arrangements, and she now tells the seller that, yes, you will qualify for the needed loan and that she will fund it. Further, she will immediately fax a new preapproval letter for the right amount.

Suddenly things look up. Your authority is better, presumably, than the one the seller's agent has. When your mortgage broker puts it all in writing, you have a solid deal. (And next time, get the right preapproval letter!)

Challenging the Authority's Credentials

There are many different cases where you'll want to challenge an authority's credentials. One of these may be when someone who, you suspect, shouldn't be butting in at all is giving you a hard time. For example, recently there was a transaction where the escrow officer kept calling me up and insisting that I produce this document or that, claiming they were essential to the transaction. At first, I complied simply to get the deal done with the least amount of hassle. But when I was asked to come up with a birth certificate, driver's license,

Social Security card number, and bank reference, I balked. The escrow officer said these were necessary to identify me in the transaction and to be sure that the check I submitted for the purchase was valid.

TRAP

In the past, if you were a buyer, simply putting a cashier's check into escrow was usually considered sufficient for completing a deal. However, in recent years some unscrupulous people have devised ways of canceling cashier's checks, and some escrows and title insurance companies have been burned by transferring title and issuing their own payment checks only to find that the buyer's cashier's check had bounced. (Believe it; it does happen!) As a consequence, today escrow agents often require additional safeguards, usually in the form of time. The cashier's check must be deposited 24 or 48 hours prior to the close of escrow so it has time to clear.

I understood the escrow officer's concerns, but realized that he was going overboard. So I said "No." I'd supply a driver's license and Social Security card number, if necessary, and deposit the cashier's check ahead of the close of escrow. That was it.

The escrow officer said that wasn't sufficient.

I replied that the escrow officer was simply there to fulfill the wishes of the parties concerned and had no authority to demand more. If he kept insisting, I'd be forced to change escrows, even at that late date.

The escrow officer was furious and called the title insurance company (to whom I was well known) and the lender. The escrow officer called back an hour later saying that he had, "smoothed things out" and the extra documents weren't really necessary after all.

Beware of people who are officious—especially those who feel is it their duty to create rules and build barriers because of their apparent position of authority. In the final analysis, they may not have the credentials to make their demands stick.

Challenge the Written Word

Have you ever noticed the power of the printed word? You're signing a lease and it says, "No pets allowed." You have a pet. Suddenly you feel the energy flowing out of the agreement. You won't get rid of Bowser and they don't take pets.

Can you keep the deal alive?

Certainly. Just remember that whoever wrote out the agreement decided that, as a general rule, pets were not desirable, and a good way of discouraging tenants from having them was to include those words. An agent can point to the sentence as proof that pets aren't allowed. You, of course, could simply cross out the word *no* and initial your change. If the landlord wanted you as a tenant, he or she might initial it too. Then pets would be allowed.

Words, when they are written, have uncommon power to affect our lives. You go to a movie theater and after buying your ticket see a sign that says, "Line forms here." So you stand there. But what if you stood somewhere else and people stood behind you. Why then the sign would be wrong, wouldn't it?

Often when filling out a mortgage application, it is noted on one or more papers that you, the borrower, are asked to sign that you must pay for a whole list of fees including:

Drawing documents

Transferring documents

Application submission fee

Administrative fee

And so on

These are, by and large, garbage fees that mortgage brokers and some lenders' representatives use to pad the profits they make from the loan. But, because it's printed on paper, most borrowers simply acquiesce without a question.

But you know that these are garbage fees and you don't want to pay them. Again, you feel the energy flowing away. Either you agree and feel cheated, or you disagree and walk out. (Not a good idea as it may cost you the deal and cause repercussions with the seller.)

There is another alternative, challenging the fees. All of these fees are challengeable and negotiable. Just because they are written down on a paper you are asked to sign doesn't mean they are non-negotiable.

TIP

When someone says that something is nonnegotiable, what they may really mean is that negotiations have just begun.

Tell the lender you want the loan, but you know these fees aren't reasonable and you want them removed or reduced. After the lender gets over his or her shock, negotiation may open. Of course, some lenders really won't dicker, particularly when they are making lots of loans. But in a slow market, many will.

Real estate documents—leases, sales agreements, options, listings—are rife with words printed to tell you what you can and cannot do. These are often called "boilerplate" because they regularly occur in every document. The trouble, of course, is that sometimes they are disadvantageous to you. For example, I was recently examining a sales agreement a builder was using that noted a minimum deposit of $5,000 was required with the offer. In other words, I had to come up with $5,000 in earnest money if I wanted to make an offer on the property.

I simply didn't want to come up with $5,000. The printed word could kill the deal.

I wrote out a check for $500 and presented it to the agent. She smiled and said I had left off a zero. I said I hadn't. She pointed to the sentence. I took her pen and crossed out the sentence, then handed her back the check for $500. She didn't smile, but she also didn't refuse to present the offer.

A friend of mine who lives out of town recently was seeking to list his property. The agent's listing agreement had written in it that the commission was 7 percent. He told the agent he was only willing to pay 4 percent.

The agent said he was sorry, but they only worked for 7 percent. My friend replied that if that was the case, he would get another agent. Eventually they compromised at 5 percent.

TIP

Just because it's written down doesn't mean it's true. If writing it down made it so, then everything you read in the newspapers would be gospel.

Make Lists

There is a corollary to this, namely that you can use the written word to your advantage. You can use the written word to add energy to a deal. When I'm presenting an offer (or having one presented to me), I like to draw up lists. I ask the buyer (or the buyer's agent) to write down everything he or she wants out of the deal. I myself make a similar list, which I hand to the other party. Of course, there are the usual things that pop up such as price and monthly payment amount. But there can often be unexpected things such as "home appearance" or "good neighborhood" or "number of bathrooms" or even "quick deal."

The list helps everyone identify what the real stumbling blocks may be. Maybe we've spent hours arguing about price. But what the buyer is really concerned about is neighborhood. If I convince the buyer that the neighborhood is really better than she thinks, she may be willing to pay a higher price. "But I'm really concerned with price," the buyer may say. "Indeed, then how come the first thing on your list is 'neighborhood'?" When it's written down, it's hard to deny.

If "quick deal" shows up anywhere on a buyer's list, I know that I'm almost home free. I simply ask, "Okay, if I'm willing to sign right now and let you move in next week, will you accept my price and terms?" I may not get everything I want this way, but I usually can get a lot of it.

Putting it in writing helps to identify the true needs and wants of the other party, which may not be revealed any other way. It also helps the other side to identify your true needs and wants. A list is a wonderful means of finding out the triggers that will make your opponent move on the deal. And giving them a list from your perspective may help them give you just what you want.

Listen Carefully

Most of us listen more to how a person talks than what he or she says. If the person is loud and speaking in an angry voice, their anger, frustration, and perhaps fear come through. If a person speaks very softly, we may suspect that he or she is very calculating and maybe even dishonest. Someone talking in a normal tone may lull us to sleep as we lose our concentration. And a person speaking with obvious conviction may convince us of their forthrightness.

The point here, however, is that no matter what the delivery is, it's often the words that count. Many times you can reenergize a deal or get negotiations moving simply by understanding what's really meant. Here are some examples:

"Here's our first offer."

This always implies that a second, third, or other better offer is to come. When I hear this phrase, I automatically feel the energy flowing because I know that if I reject it, the second offer will be forthcoming.

"This is our initial bid."

Again, better things to come later; see above.

"Here's something to get negotiations back on track."

This is a concession. Why would the other party offer up a concession without receiving something in return, unless he is more desperate to get the deal than I am? I will accept the concession and then see what happens next.

"Let's get things out on the table."

This implies to me that I'm only going to see the negotiating position, not the final offer. The other side is presenting what he wants me to see. Now I'll show him what I want him to see. Then we'll get to it.

"This is our first and final offer."

Maybe, but only a fool issues an ultimatum at the start of negotiations. Is the other party really that stupid? Or is she trying to stampede me into giving concessions? Now is when I should get her to invest time in the deal. (See Chapter 2.)

"This is the best offer we can make."

Come on now, everyone can always do better. This comment is usually made by real estate agents about their clients. What it usually means is that this is the offer the agent got without a lot of hassle. It's often a prelude to real concessions and negotiations.

"Take it or leave it!"

This statement is usually issued after lengthy negotiations. Unless it's a ploy to force action on my part, it usually means the other side is frustrated and has decided it's better to give up the deal than continue trying to come up with something mutually acceptable. If I take it, I usually lose. If I leave it, we both usually lose. The better course is to ask for a short break, then come back and note areas of agreement, identify those of disagreement, and find a spot where some negotiation seems possible.

I think you get the idea. The words the other party says are very revealing, if only you listen to them.

TIP

Beware of delivery, listen closely to content. Sometimes it's not just the specific words themselves, but their sum total. For example, how should you respond to the following situation in negotiating?

You're a buyer asking a seller to carry back a second mortgage on the property. You must have this second mortgage to make the deal. However, the seller offers questions such as:

"Is the interest rate high enough?"

"What if you lose your job and can't make the payments?"

"During the last recession there were a lot of defaults on second mortgages, weren't there?"

"I hear that sellers are often cheated by creative financing."

What is this seller saying? For one thing, she's not saying that she doesn't want a second mortgage. If she didn't want a second mortgage, she would say, "No." Instead, in each statement she's saying, "Yes, but . . ." It's the "but" that we need to address.

If we simply answer the questions without listening to what's actually being said, we might respond in this fashion: "The interest rate is as high as the market will bear; I've been on my job for five years and prospects look good; yes, there were a lot of defaults, but the recession is over; creative financing isn't always bad—sometimes it's a good way to make a deal."

Have we responded in a way that will get the seller to go along? I suspect not. If we listen more closely to what the seller is saying, we might perceive that she is really concerned that she will lose a lot of money or be cheated by taking a second mortgage. When she asks if the interest rate is high "enough," she's not asking about market rates, but whether it's enough to warrant the personal risk to her. When she asks what happens if I "can't make" the payments, she doesn't want to hear about my job. She wants to know that I'll make the payments no matter what. When she asks about "defaults," she wants to know what's going to happen to her if I don't pay. And "cheated" suggests she doesn't trust anything that I'm saying about this subject.

The words reveal the true problem. What the seller really needs is to be reassured. What will reassure her? One sure thing is if I increase my credibility as a borrower. For example, perhaps I could get someone financially well established (such as my parents, a wealthy relative, even the broker) to cosign. Or I could increase credibility if I'm able to put more money down.

Once I've done something like this to reassure the seller of my credibility, the arguments (in the form of questions) that she's raised melt away. She might even be willing to give me a lower than market interest rate and be sufficiently unconcerned about payments, defaults, or cheating to make concessions elsewhere.

What I have to do is listen to the words and discover the true concerns they reveal. Once I address these concerns, the superficial problems will dissolve.

Listen to the words. They will usually tell you what the other party really wants.

The Bottom Line

Learn to act.

Disarm a psychological attack by drawing attention to it.

Be irrational occasionally.

Strive to be innocent.

Always ask "Why?"

Question authority.

Challenge the written word.

Listen carefully.

5
Walk Away
a Winner

I originally titled this chapter, "Common Sense." But everyone always tells you to use common sense in everything you do, and it's almost impossible to tie it down to specifics. On the other hand, looking for a way to make things work involves action that is doable. It gives you a target to aim for. In real estate, the best deals are often made when people get creative. In this chapter, we'll look at six commonsense approaches that will help you to make negotiating work.

Always Give Yourself an Alternative

This rule is all about leverage in negotiation. If you follow it, you'll have leverage. If you don't, you will not get the deal you want because you won't have the leverage necessary to get it.

The classic example here is of a young couple who go out to buy their first home. They are shown dozens of properties, until one day they run across one that's simply perfect. It's got location: close to shopping, safe neighborhood, and near schools. The house has the right number of bedrooms and bathrooms. The design of the kitchen is perfect, the arrangement of the rooms delightful. In short, it's the one house of their dreams. And therein lies the rub.

Our couple has found the right house, the perfect house, the one and only house, and they have no alternative. Thus, when the seller asks $25,000 more than its market value, what are they to do?

Yes, they can bluff and offer less. But even this option is limited because they are so worried that someone will come in with a higher offer and snatch it out from under them. Thus, when the seller rejects a first lower offer, in order not to lose this perfect property, they give the seller exactly what he wants—not only in price, but in terms as well.

In short, the buyers have no leverage with which to negotiate. They must have the house. Consequently, they have to pay the price.

On the other hand, consider a more mature couple. They have bought and sold a number of homes. They are now looking for their next home, and in the process, they identify three homes within a given neighborhood that are all suitable. They pick the best of the lot and make an offer, perhaps $25,000 less than the asking price.

When the seller counters with only a thousand dollars less than he's asking, the couple doesn't at all feel they have to take it or lose out on the one and only property of their dreams. They know there are two other perfectly good houses waiting for their offer. So they tell the seller that either he can take their original offer or they'll look elsewhere. Further, they only give him 24 hours to decide.

Suddenly the seller realizes that if he's going to sell to this couple, he'll have to lower his sights. If the market's toughened, if there haven't been any other buyers (in other words, the seller doesn't have any alternatives), if he needs to get out, he may indeed take the buyers' lowball offer. At the very least, he's likely to make a more realistic counter.

TIP

Houses are like love. Either you believe there is one and only one perfect mate for you in the whole world, or you come to realize that you can be perfectly happy with hundreds, perhaps thousands, of different people who are all "just right," if you can find them. Similarly, you can believe there is only one perfect house in the world for you. Or you can be more pragmatic and realize that there are dozens, even hundreds, of homes in which you could be perfectly happy. The pragmatic person can negotiate. The perfectionist has to pay the price that's asked.

The need for alternatives applies not only to the purchase of a home, but also to all aspects of real estate, whether it's finding suitable financing, negotiating a lease, or simply paying a deposit. If you give yourself options, you will be in a position to negotiate. If you leave yourself no alternatives, you are more likely to have to accept whatever the other party offers.

Be Informed

TIP

The old maxim "Knowledge is power" applies doubly in real estate.

Being informed can make a big difference in almost every sale. For example, you're presenting an offer that contains a financing contingency that specifies that the purchase is subject to your obtaining a 90 percent of value mortgage. (You're putting 10 percent down.)

As soon as you present your offer, the agent for the seller says, "You can't get that loan because you're not planning to live in the property. Only buyers who intend to live in the home can get a 90 percent loan. The best investors can get is 80 or maybe 75 percent mortgages. Either come up with more down or you've got no deal!"

Now, do you look wide-eyed, confused, and slightly embarrassed by this turn of events? If you do, then you haven't done your homework. Further, you're not going to be able to negotiate successfully here unless you come up with a lot more money, which you probably don't want to do (or are unable to do). The problem is that you don't know the right answer.

You should previously have contacted lenders or a good mortgage broker to find out if a non-owner-occupied purchase would qualify for 90 percent financing. (It seldom does!) If there's no financing available, then you should have structured your offer differently, perhaps with a 75 percent first loan and a 15 percent second from the seller.

Or, you should have found a lender who will give you a nonoccupant 90 percent mortgage. (A few do exist in some areas.)

If you had done your homework and been properly informed, when challenged by the seller's agent, you could have simply smiled and whipped out a preapproval letter from a lender promising to make you a 90 percent loan on the property. The seller's agent would now look foolish (instead of you) and you might be able to press for some other concessions, having thus established your authority.

Or, can you imagine this happening? You're a seller receiving an offer to purchase a property that contains a contingency clause. (A contingency is simply a condition that must be met before the sale can be completed.) The clause says, "Seller agrees to pay for all costs of repair or retrofitting as required by termite or other reports as required by lender, insurer, or state."

Now, should you sign a contract with this contingency in it or not? You may know that virtually all lenders require at least a termite report clearance before they will fund a mortgage for the buyer. Also, in almost all locales the seller is expected to pay for correcting all damage. You're prepared for this. But, are there any other reports that are required? If so, then this could add up to a lot of money and you may want to delete the condition. If not, and the buyer is just being cautious, you may want to go ahead and sign. The question is one of knowledge.

Many people, figuring this only applies to a termite report and clearance for which they have to pay anyway, would sign. However, in some areas today there are additional requirements now being made by the lender, insurer, or the state. For example, some states may soon require that an earthquake, hurricane, or cyclone report be issued and that a clearance showing the house is protected from these be given prior to sale. The costs here can be extremely high, perhaps in the range of $20,000 per house or more. If you sign, you could be committed to making the corrections.

Or perhaps the lender may require a special report on flooding because you are in a flood plain, as well as a clearance showing that certain expensive retrofitting steps have been taken to protect your home. Or a fire insurance company may require a report on roofs in your area because of an extreme fire hazard where your property is located. The insurer may also insist on a clearance saying that your roof is of fireproof materials before issuing insurance. (Replacing an old wood shingle roof with fireproof shingles or tiles can easily cost $15,000 or more.)

TRAP

Some sellers simply don't realize that everything in an offer is negotiable, including the contingencies. If you don't like the contingency, you can rewrite it. Of course, that nullifies the offer and now you must get the buyer to accept your changes. But that's all part of the negotiation.

Today the whole world of real estate transactions is complicated by the demands of a host of companies and agencies that are external to the transaction. However, if you're unaware of what's required of you in your area, your ignorance could cost you a fortune. If you sign a clause saying you'll pay, then you'll probably have to pay.

TIP

Although signed sales agreements are supposed to be binding, in actual practice, the language in them is often flawed or the sellers or buyers can claim they were not properly informed about the consequences of their actions by their agents or attorney. Thus, another useful bit of knowledge is that just because you signed doesn't necessarily mean you're always on the hook. Extenuating circumstances just might save your rear end. Only you can't count on this. It's far better to have the knowledge you need to avoid signing a bad agreement than to sign and have to try to get out of it later on.

The key here is to be informed. Having knowledge of pertinent facts can often mean the difference between negotiating a winning or a losing deal.

Only Work on Issues
That Can Be Resolved

TIP

Always do the possible first. Leave the impossible till later.

You're a buyer and you offer to purchase a home. You want the seller to accept a lower price, carry a second mortgage, move out within 30 days, and put on a new roof. When the seller looks at this list, her first inclination is to throw it and you out the door.

But you want to buy and she wants to sell. So you suggest that first you both identify any issues that can be resolved and separate them from those that can't.

Price comes up immediately. She doesn't want to accept what you are offering, but indicates she will negotiate something lower than she's asking. There is a possible resolution here.

Next she mentions that she doesn't want to put on a new roof. But she knows that the old roof is bad and is willing to patch it. Maybe that's negotiable too.

However, she flat out says she cannot move out in 30 days. She simply can't. Her kids are in school for another two and a half months. She would have to find another place to live and is going to be traveling for the next month, so she won't have time to look. It's simply not possible. This issue is intractable. Further, she says she needs cash, so in no way will she consider a second mortgage. Again, intractable.

Now, are you going to focus on the time factor and the second mortgage? Or on the roof and the price? If you turn to the time factor, she says, "No, No, No." If you turn to the issue of the second mortgage, again she says, "No, No, No." Suddenly it appears as if everything is wrong and there's no way to move forward. In fact, you've just lost the deal because you've brought negotiations to a halt.

On the other hand, if you instead concentrate on the two issues that may be possible to resolve, maybe you can make some progress. So you work with the seller on the roof. No, she doesn't want to replace it, but she concedes it is bad. Eventually you both agree that she'll put on a new roof, but a less expensive one.

You both heave a sigh of relief. Things are going better. You've just resolved a big issue. The time you've both invested has paid off. You're both optimistic. So you now tackle price.

"Your offer is too low," she says. But she concedes that she has some room to maneuver. "How much room?" you ask. You continue to negotiate into the wee hours of the night and finally hit upon a price that both of you consider reasonable, and again a collective sigh of relief is expressed. You both feel you're much closer to a deal.

But, you point out, you can't give that price unless the seller gives you a second mortgage. You don't have the extra cash. But, she says, she must have the cash in order to buy the next house.

So, you put your heads together to see what you can work out. You suggest that she take that second mortgage and sell it to an investor. No, she won't get full price for it. But if you're a good credit risk (and you surely indicate you are), if the interest rate is high enough, and the term is short enough, couldn't she convert it to cash somewhere? Her ears prick up. She says, "Maybe there is a way."

She remembers an uncle with a lot of cash who's looking for solid investments. She rousts her uncle out of bed, even though it's 12:30 a.m., makes effusive apologies for the late call, and then explains the problem. The uncle, convinced of the severity of the problem by the late hour call, but always looking for a good deal and liking his niece, agrees. He'll sign off in the morning.

You both shake hands. It appears you've got the deal. "Oh, by the way," you mention. "I still need to move in within 30 days."

"No problem," says the seller. "I'll move out and rent temporarily." The deal is done.

But, why is it done?

The answer is that it's human nature to "go with the flow," to follow the trend. The word is *momentum*. Get it on your side and you can make a seemingly impossible deal.

You can see this most clearly in basketball games. You may have two evenly matched teams, but if one gains momentum by quickly building up a lead, the game may blow out and become a mismatched contest. Similarly, in a real estate deal, once movement begins to occur, once you have agreement on some issues, the tendency is to want to continue the momentum, to continue finding agreement (just as, if there were no momentum, the tendency would be to feel the deal had no chance of being made). Agreement begets agreement—it's positive action. In the end, an issue such as when to give occupancy, which is intractable at the beginning, seems trivial after everything else has been accomplished.

TIP

If you work first on those issues that you can resolve, those which you can't may take care of themselves.

Remember, if you begin by trying to negotiate an impossible issue, you are doomed to failure. So why bother? Instead, work on those issues that you can resolve. Maybe, just maybe, by the time you've successfully worked out several issues, the other party will have enough familiarity with you and confidence in you and the negotiating process to make concessions that seemed impossible hours earlier.

TRAP

Some readers unfamiliar with just how real estate deals are put together may not believe anyone would make a call at 12:30 in the morning asking for money, much less get it. Believe it! When a seller (or buyer) is hot to close a deal, he or she will do almost anything to make the deal work.

Never Respond to an Offer That Can't Be Closed

This is a real estate classic. You're a seller and are asking $200,000 for your property. A buyer comes through your house, looks at it, leaves, and then the next day comes back again. You're sure this person is interested and, after talking a while, she says, "Would you take $160,000 for your property?"

You're anxious to sell and you reply, "No, no I wouldn't, but I'd look favorably at $185,000!"

You've just committed a "no-no!" You've started negotiations on a deal that can't be concluded. Why can't it be concluded? Because there's no formal offer on the table. The would-be buyer hasn't offered anything. She has simply asked a question.

In effect, you've just given away $15,000 before the negotiations have even begun. If this would-be buyer eventually makes an offer, you can be darn sure it's going to be predicated on an asking price of $185,000, not the $200,000 you purportedly want.

What should you have said? That's easy. When the would-be buyers ask, "Would you take $160,000 for your property?" The correct reply is, "Are you offering $160,000?"

The would-be buyer might now fall back and regroup. "Well, let's say that I do? Would you consider it?"

This is merely a restatement of the first question. You now need to restate your response.

"Put your offer in writing, enclose an earnest money deposit, present it to me, and I'll let you know."

The point is that that you should only respond to a legitimate offer that can be closed. If it can't be closed, then true negotiations haven't really started.

TIP

Your goal is to get the other party to the negotiating table. Until an offer is made, you've got nothing to negotiate.

TRAP

According to the Statute of Frauds, real estate sales agreements must be in writing to be valid.

Time Outs

This problem can crop up at any time. For example, you've made an offer to a seller and are hot in negotiations. Along the way the seller suddenly says, "What if we just table this for a while? I think you need to go back and rethink your offer, and I need to sleep on it."

TRAP

You don't "table" real estate negotiations. Either you've got a deal . . . or you haven't.

What the seller is actually proposing here is to stop negotiations. In effect, he's making an offer that can't be closed. If you accept, you allow your offer to continue in force indefinitely while he neither accepts nor rejects it. In other words, he's asking for an open-ended offer on your part. If a better offer comes in over the course of the next few days or weeks, he's free to take it. (By the way, in real estate, all offers are presented as they arrive. Even if you have an offer pending, if another is made, it is, or should be, presented immediately.) The seller here has nothing to lose if you agree. He is, in effect, offering you nothing.

The point, of course, is that the seller is making an open-ended offer that can't be closed. Your response should be immediate and clear. You might say something like, "I understand what you're saying. But I'm looking to buy property today, and I have several pieces I'm considering. I believe we should continue negotiations until they are concluded. If you break them off, I'll assume that's a rejection and look elsewhere." Be friendly, indicate you have alternatives, and lead the negotiations back toward a conclusion.

Don't Stick to the "Pie" Analogy or "Bottom Line" Reasoning

Sometime in the distant past there was an unlucky baker who said, "I've only got so many pieces of pie to sell and when they're gone, I'll close for the day." Soon after, "pie charts" came into existence for demonstrating how the total amount in a transaction could be distributed, and we were all locked into an unfortunate analogy. When it became common practice to speak of this as the "bottom line," meaning that this was the last position we would take on a deal, negotiation took a giant step backward.

The Problem with Pie

On the surface, this appears to be a sound analogy. A deal, any deal, only has so much money (or property or conditions or whatever). That means that, like a pie, it can only be cut into so many pieces. Each person in the deal can get a big slice or a small slice. But when all the slices are handed out, the pie is gone.

You want to buy a home, but you're offering much less than the seller is asking. When you present the deal and begin negotiating, the seller brings up the pie analogy. He says, "You're offering $200,000 for the property. I have to pay a 6 percent commission or $12,000. I have a $150,000 first mortgage and a $30,000 second mortgage. That leaves me only $8,000, out of which I have to pay closing costs. By the time the deal is done, I won't have any money left at all! I won't sign."

So long as we hold to the pie analogy, he's perfectly correct and there's no deal to be made here. However, let's throw the pie back at the baker and work creatively. What about the furniture? Maybe there's some nice furniture in the house that originally cost the seller $10,000. But he's moving to an apartment and doesn't have room for most of it. Indeed, he's tired of it and would be happy to sell it. So you offer an additional $5,000 for the furniture. He's happy to get rid of it and now he's got some cash. In addition, you up the price to $205,000, and if the lender concurs, you finance the cost so it's only pennies a month out of your pocket. The pie's gotten bigger.

Maybe the seller has other assets—an RV vehicle for example. You've always wanted one of these, indeed had planned on buying one. So instead of buying just property, you buy the property and the RV. He gets more cash, which is what he wants, and you get something you would have bought anyway. The pie's growing again.

The real estate agent wants to make the deal. But maybe there's no deal without some creative concessions. So instead of $12,000 in cash, you ask the agent to take $5,000 in cash and a second mortgage on another property owned by the seller. He pays the agent off a little each month, but gets to keep $7,000 in cash for himself.

The pie's bigger still.

TRAP

 Don't expect a real estate agent to automatically offer to discount a commission by taking back paper (mortgage) instead of cash. Most won't want to do it. Many simply won't do it at all. But, creative agents who do a lot of business and see that the deal can't be made any other way often will. It's usually a last resort kind of thing. But, when it works, it can make the deal.

There's really no limit to how big you can grow the pie, once you stop seeing it as a limiting analogy.

Bottom Lining

Now, let's move from the conceptual image of a pie to a specific application. Many people, particularly those who don't negotiate regularly, feel it's important to adopt a "bottom line." They see this as a safety precaution to keep them from committing too deeply or spending to much. It's like going to Las Vegas and saying, "We've got $300 to blow. When it's all gone, we quit." In other words, they are committing to a pie of a certain maximum size in advance.

There's really nothing wrong with doing this. Indeed, so long as you understand its limitations, it's often a good idea. The real trouble with setting up a bottom line, however, is that you usually do it before you understand the whole deal. And once the entire deal is presented to you, you may find that the bottom line set is inappropriate.

For example, Peter and Sheila are selling their home. They're asking $395,000. However, they know that offers are most likely to come in for less. So before hand, they decide the minimum they'll accept. They decide it's $365,000. If they can't get $365,000, they won't sell.

There are two things wrong here. First, what if an offer comes in for exactly $365,000? That's their bottom line. Do they accept the offer? Or do they hold out for more?

They are at a psychological disadvantage if they've already decided that $365,000 is their bottom line. They are thinking that here's an offer they can accept. If they counter, they are giving up this offer in the hope (perhaps vain hope) that they'll get more.

Maybe it's better to take one in the hand than two in the bush? Having already set up a bottom line, they are unlikely to counter, or if they do, to counter weakly. In short, their bottom line may get them less than they might otherwise have gotten for their home.

On the other hand, let's say the offer comes in at $335,000. Now, they know they won't accept that offer no matter what. In fact, it's way off the mark and they may feel insulted. They may only make a token counter, which could make the buyer feel it's hopeless and cause him or her to give up on the deal.

Or maybe they'll counter at their bottom line, $365,000. Now, when the buyer counters back at $360,000, what do they do? They've got nowhere to go. In this case, their bottom line has restricted their flexibility to deal with a lowball offer.

On the other hand, let's say that Peter and Sheila did not set up a bottom line. The first offer comes in at $335,000. They might come back with a higher counteroffer. They want the most they can get and are willing to negotiate for it.

What about the $335,000 offer? Maybe they'll examine the terms the buyer is offering. Perhaps there's a second mortgage for them with a very high interest rate involved that they like. Maybe, because of the terms, they'll accept $360,000 or $355,000 or even $350,000.

The point here is that if you set a bottom line in advance, you limit your ability to negotiate. It's like the pie analogy all over again. You've locked yourself in and have nowhere to go.

TRAP

 The bottom line is supposed to protect you from losing more than you want or are able to afford. However, just as often, it keeps you from getting a deal or making more than you anticipated.

The simple truth is that you can't know what your true best bottom line is in advance. Only when you see the deal, its terms, and its ramifications can you decide what's in your best interests. Therefore, my suggestion is that if you feel the need for a bottom line, make it tentative, not rigid.

TIP

Say to yourself, "This is what I'd like to get without seeing the deal. However, I'll rethink it after I see the deal
itself."

Remember That Some Deals Can't Be Made— No Matter What

I've been asked why I included this in a list of rules for successful
negotiations. The reason is that unless you recognize in the back of
your mind that sometimes the deal can't be made, you will miss out
on some good deals.

Sometimes, but only after extensive, intensive, and forthright
negotiation, it becomes clear that no matter what you do, you can't
make a deal with the other party. You've been careful and have not
offended the other side; you're dealing with a person who has the
power to negotiate; you've made lists; you've disarmed psychological
attacks. You've done it all. And after all of it, the deal just can't seem
to be made. You're too far apart in price or in terms. You've tried to
compromise. You realize the other side has tried to compromise.
The awful truth is that there just isn't a deal to be made here.

Once you realize this, the mistake is to continue negotiating. If
you continue, you may give up something you can't afford to lose
and may end up with a deal you're better off without.

TRAP

What's worse than not making a deal? It's making a
deal in which you lose.

What you do is announce that you've tried your best. You've given
it every bit of creative effort you have and you just don't see how any
deal can be made between the two of you. So, you're ending negotiations. If you're a buyer, you'll look for another house. If you're a
seller, you'll look for another buyer.

At this point, the other side has a decision to make. Either he or she can concur with you, shake hands, say there's no hard feelings, and leave, each of you to go your separate ways.

Or, he or she can make concessions that will make the deal more appealing to you.

Why would a buyer or seller do this?

One reason may be that this person has been giving you only the posture, the negotiating "position," and that he or she really does want to make this work very badly. By walking away from the table, you've forced it out into the open.

Another reason may be that this person has never read this book and simply doesn't know that sometimes it's better not to make the deal. He or she is determined to make the deal no matter what, even if it's at a disadvantage.

TRAP

Sometimes people will walk away from negotiations as a ploy. It's not that they believe no deal can be made. They think they can pressure the other side into making concessions. However, if you walk away before concluding there is no deal possible—if you do it as a ploy—how do you come back if the other side recognizes what you're doing and simply says, "Bye-bye"? If you still want the deal, now you have to come back, eat humble pie, and try again from an obviously weaker position.

The ultimate test of the other side is to conclude that there's no deal to be made and walk away. If they let you go, then you know that your assessment was correct. If, however, they rush after you urging you to come back to the table, then you now know that they've only been posturing, not really being fully open.

When you're called back, it's time to play hardball. You can say the obvious, "I walked away because I assumed there was nothing more to say or do. But your calling me back suggests that my understanding of what you have to offer was incorrect. What are you now bringing to this deal that is new and will cause me to continue with the negotiations?"

Often the other side will now present some new concession or creative plan. However, I have been in this position and had the opposite side simply reiterate their old position. As soon as it became apparent that nothing new was offered, I walked away again. When they came after me once more, I simply said, "Put it in writing and I'll consider it," and left.

TRAP

You can't negotiate successfully with people whose main hope of "winning" is simply to wear you down by keeping you at the table.

TIP

If the other side is a "wear 'em out" negotiator, do it at a distance. Get them to write it down on paper and submit it to you at your home or work. You can then accept, reject, or modify. By maintaining distance you have avoided having the other side gain an advantage by wearing you out.

Walking Away a Winner Is No Baloney

The gospel of negotiators has always been that a good deal means that both sides win. I get what I want and you get what you want.

However, this does not mean that each side comes away with what they wanted at the beginning or that one side doesn't come away with a lot more than the other. It means that the purpose of the negotiation is to get everything out on the table and to balance it all so that both parties can see what an equitable settlement is.

Sometimes, more often than not, one party will not even realize what it really wants or how strongly it wants it until negotiations are heated. Then, suddenly, the seller decides that she's got to have 90 days before moving and is willing to make concessions on price and terms to get it. Or the buyer decides he's got to have that chandelier from the seller, even if it means paying more for the house.

That's why it may appear to an outsider that one side has come away with more than another. In a truly successful negotiation, however, there was a just scale on which all things were balanced. And in the balance, whether to an onlooker it looked as though one party got 90 percent and the other 10 percent, to the parties concerned—because of their strength of need or feeling—it was strictly a 50–50, win–win deal.

That's what negotiations are really all about—finding a way to give the other side what it wants so that you can get what you need.

The Bottom Line

In order to walk away a winner:

Always give yourself an alternative.

Be informed.

Only work on issues that can be resolved.

Never respond to an offer that can't be closed.

Don't stick to the "pie" analogy or "bottom line."

Remember that some deals can't be made, no matter what.

6

How to Win
a Bidding War

In a hot market, there are typically far more buyers than sellers. As a result, prices are moving up. Indeed, in a very hot market, sellers may get two, three, or more offers for their property, often for more than the asking price, within days of listing it. It's great for the sellers, not so great for buyers.

But what if you're a buyer? How are you going to get that home? How are you going to knock down that seller's price? What must you do to be sure you don't overpay?

If you're a seller, how do you get buyers into a bidding frenzy? How do you make sure your initial asking price isn't too low?

Getting your price in a competitive market for buyers may mean paying more than the next person, but not too much more. For sellers, it may mean pricing it higher, or lower, than it seems the house is worth.

First we'll talk about buyer strategies. Then, we'll move on to seller tactics.

Buyers—Load Your Weapons

If you're a buyer in a hot seller's market, you need to arm yourself for negotiating warfare. You have four weapons at your disposal, and all of them must be ready.

Market Knowledge:
What Should the Home Sell For?

In order to be competitive in a seller's market, a buyer must know the market. My suggestion is that before you make an offer, you spend weekends touring with an agent(s) looking at homes for sale. Get to know what's available and what it should cost. That way, when a home comes up for sale, you won't need to waste time trying to determine whether or not it's priced fairly, too high, or too low. You'll know because of your experience in looking at other homes. Also, read the real estate sections of several local newspapers. Find out what the columnists say about the market.

Talk with at least three different agents, not about specific properties (although that will certainly come up), but about sales. How have they been? How fast is the turnover of houses in the multiple listing service? (Anything over five or six months is considered high and indicates a slow market. Anything under 60 days indicates a hot market.) Are sellers getting their prices, or are homes selling far below "asking"? Are multiple offers on homes a common occurrence? Or do houses sit for months with no interest in them? Prepare your offer accordingly.

Financing Knowledge:
How Much Can You Spend?

It doesn't matter if you can get a home for a piddling $175,000 if you can't get a big enough mortgage to cover that amount. Talk with at least one mortgage broker. Get yourself preapproved. Today a preapproval letter is no longer a plus; it's a necessity. Expect all competitors for the home to have one. Once you know the maximum you can afford, you can bid more realistically.

Have your cash for the down payment and closing costs in hand. And be sure that your mortgage broker is ready to fax you a preapproval letter for *just the amount of financing you need* (and can get) for the special deal you want. (The letter shouldn't be for more than you're offering. The seller will immediately see you can afford more . . . and may ask for more.)

Personal Knowledge:
What Are Your Alternatives?

The key to any kind of effective negotiating strategy is to have alternatives. If you don't get this house, can you get that other one? The worst position to be in is to feel that this is the only house in the world for you. If you feel that way, then almost certainly you'll pay too much.

TRAP

If you have alternatives, it will be easier for you to walk away when the bidding gets too high. Sometimes buyers involved in a bidding war become irrational. They stop making sound judgments and get caught up in just winning. Having alternatives helps keep you from falling into this trap.

Some agents suggest that you rate the house on a scale of 1 to 10 with 10 being the ideal home for you. (Remember, that "ideal" is a very lofty goal.) If the home rates a 5 or 6, then you'll certainly bid differently than if it's a 9 or 10.

Seller Knowledge:
What's the Seller's Motivation?

There can be a hundred different reasons why a seller wants out of a property. The exact reason itself isn't necessarily important. What is important is how much pressure that reason puts on the seller.

For example, a seller faced with a job transfer, loss of income, or even foreclosure is going to be highly motivated. That seller will be anxious to conclude a sale. On the other hand, a seller who is employed and who simply wants to move up to a larger home is likely to be less motivated. This seller may be far more willing to refuse to negotiate a lower price no matter what you say or offer. The motivation simply isn't there.

TIP

Real estate agents are always talking about "motivated sellers." A highly motivated seller is one who has to get out soon, or even immediately. A seller who lacks motivation can simply sit on the property and wait for the right deal to come in. Smart buyers don't just look for a good property; they also look for the highly motivated seller.

Of course, the really tricky part about motivation is finding out what it is. Occasionally a seller who is highly motivated will instruct his or her agent to broadcast that fact as far and as loudly as possible. "Tell everybody I'm motivated. Bring in those deals!"

But sometimes this is just a ploy to get buyers to make offers. The seller is trying to convert those buyer hopes into higher prices through a bidding war.

TRAP

If, as a seller, you tell people you are highly motivated, you will get more offers. But the offers might be of lower quality. And you might have greater difficulty in negotiating a higher price because the buyers you attract will tend to be only those looking for a "steal."

Ask your agent if he or she knows the seller's motivation. Often agents will snoop around and get a good idea of why the seller wants out.

How Do I Handle a Bidding War?

In very hot markets it may turn out that even though you act as quickly as you can, other buyers are doing the same thing. Thus, suddenly you find that there are multiple offers on the very property you want. If that happens, what should you do?

There's an old Chinese adage that goes something like, "Sometimes the only way to win is not to compete." Consider picking up your marbles and going elsewhere. In bidding wars, often it's only the seller who wins. If you remember that there are always going to be other homes, you may find the strength to bow out gracefully and let others pay too much for the home.

On the other hand, if you've done your homework, you may realize that the real reason for the bidding war is that the home was underpriced to begin with. If that's the case, you may want to continue with the negotiation, up to what you consider a fair price. If you have a sharp pencil, you might find that you can pay more than asking and still get the home for a good price.

Bidding Madness.   Sometimes, however, a kind of bidding fever sets in that causes buyers to bid prices up beyond market value. This irrationality means that the "winner" ends up a loser with a house that costs more than he could turn around and sell it for. As I said, the best way to win here is not to compete.

Negotiating in a Hot Market

If you're a buyer in a very hot market, here are some tactics you can use to get the house you want.

Act Quickly.   It's the early bird that gets the worm in a hot market. Often if your offer gets there before others, particularly if you're a day or more ahead, and have the financing all arranged (see above), the seller may accept it. Wait and competing offers may come in, some better than yours.

Show That You're the Better Buyer.   Use a preapproval letter specifically designed for your offer.

Write a Letter to the Seller.   Used increasingly in bidding situations, the buyers explain why they should get the home. If you use this tool, don't whine and don't complain. Talk about how much you like the house, how it would be a good place for the kids to live, why it's close to work, and how you would cherish it. Don't get too mushy, but try to win over the seller's sympathy. Maybe they were once a young couple like yourselves, hoping to get into a home they could barely afford. Maybe they'll pick your offer over a better offer because they like you.

Jump the Price.   If warranted by market values, make your bid significantly higher than the competition. If your house is priced at $500,000 and there are other bidders, come in at $520,000. It tends to freeze out the competition, who suddenly see you as a "big roller" against whom they can't compete. Just remember, don't go over market value.

TRAP

In competitive bidding, the buyers are not supposed to know what the other offers are. However, very often agents get this information and pass it along.

Insist That Your Offer Be Presented in Person.   In hot markets, agents tend to just fax in offers. That doesn't do you any good. Your agent's making a fat commission on the sale if it goes through. The least he or she can do is insist on presenting the offer in person. This makes an impression on the sellers, particularly if the agent can give your offer a "face" by delivering to the seller your letter that explains who you are and why getting this house is so important to you.

Try a Deadline.   When there are multiple offers, sellers will often sit back and take their time deciding, hoping that even more and better offers will arrive. Make your offer the best one and then insist the seller give a "yea" or "nay" immediately. If the seller refuses, consider moving on.

Locate the "Lost" Seller.   In some markets, your agent will explain that your offer can't be presented because the seller is "out of town and unavailable." Some sellers will "list and leave," coming back a week or two later to, hopefully, a bunch of offers. The truth is that anyone on this planet can be reached in a few hours by phone, fax, FedEx, or some other means . . . unless they don't want to be reached. If that's the case, then look for another deal since you've got no seller to work with.

Buyers—Look for Fixers

As a buyer, one way to sometimes get a lower price is to find a lesser quality house. Just as not all peaches are created equal, neither are all properties. Ripe, round peaches with a fresh aroma and a perfect skin (no bruises) will command top dollar. Houses that are located in desirable neighborhoods, have a view, are close to an amenity such as a golf course or lake, and show well likewise command top dollar. On the other hand, properties that are rundown and in less desired neighborhoods can't command that high price.

All of this is to say that if you are buying a "bruised" property, you are more likely to be able to negotiate a lower price than if you are buying a property perfect in all aspects. This holds true regardless of the market conditions or the seller's motivation.

TRAP

It does not mean that a great house in a great location will always sell for a great price. It just means that, in any given market, such a house should bring top dollar and sell faster than a house in a lesser neighborhood that doesn't show nearly as well.

As noted, you should at least roughly be able to determine the quality of any given house if you have spent some time looking at the market. Very quickly you will come to know which neighborhoods are more desired and which less. The seller or agent will immediately let you know about any special feature, such as a view or proximity to a golf course. And your own eyes will tell you if the house has terrific "curb appeal."

If you determine that the house you are buying (or selling) is a real peach, then for any given market you should expect there will be more and better offers. If, on the other hand, the house needs paint and clean up (or more serious rehabilitation), the neighborhood is a dump, and the house sticks right out on a corner lot between two heavily traveled streets, then, buying or selling, expect fewer offers at lower prices.

Of course, if you're the buyer and you get a "steal" on a ragged-looking house, just remember that you'll need to fix it up. But at least you'll be in a home.

Sellers—Stick to Your Guns

In a hot market, as a seller you want to get the highest price you can. That means using a variety of strategies, some sound . . . some not so sound. First off, however, you need to know just what your home is worth.

To find out, do as buyers do—become a "pretend buyer" for a few weekends and, with your agent, go out and see what your competition is. You'll quickly come to see market value. Also, have your agent prepare a CMA (comparative market analysis), which should give you an excellent idea of where the price *was*.

Understand "Forward Pricing"

If there are multiple bids on a home, you have to ask yourself, "Was it originally priced too low?" I would argue that, yes, that's often the case. The home was actually priced under market, hence the competitive bidding.

Think of it this way. Prices in your area are moving up by 10 percent a year (or 20 percent or whatever). The last home that sold in the neighborhood went for $300,000 six months ago. What is a similar home worth today?

If you answered $300,000, or even $305,000, you'd be wrong. It's probably worth $315,000. That's pricing it forward to the current market.

The reason, of course, is price inflation. If prices are moving up 10 percent a year, then in half a year they've moved up 5 percent. If the home was worth $300,000 six months ago, based on comparable sales, then it's worth 5 percent more today, or $315,000. At that price, it should move quickly with full-price offers. (If there are competitive bids, then prices are moving up even faster, and you should ask more.)

Don't simply take what the last home in the neighborhood sold for and make that your price. Forward pricing is based on inflation. You can find out what your local market is doing by checking local newspapers. They often run stories on housing price increases. You can also check with www.dqnews.com and other online pricing services for pricing info.

TRAP

 A home may be selling for more than the highest price previously achieved in a neighborhood and still be underpriced.

Purposely Underpricing

Some agents will suggest to sellers that they purposely underprice a home in order to start a bidding war. It works like this: Instead of forward pricing your home at the current market price of $800,000, you instead price it at $750,000 (or some other lower figure).

Buyers learning of an underpriced home may immediately come looking and start making offers. Then, you as a seller simply sit back and hold off making a selling decision for a few weeks until the buying frenzy has forced the price up above the $800,000 mark. You get a quick sale . . . and for more money.

Unless . . . no buyers show up. Or unless buyers show up and make full price offers at only your below market price. No, you don't have to sell in that circumstance, but you might still owe a commission to the agent.

Yes, underpricing can work—unless it works against you.

The Bottom Line

In a hot real estate market, knowledge is king. Know what the home is worth. And negotiate for all you're worth.

7
Negotiate the Commission

I have a good friend who to this day is fond of recalling the first time he ever listed a house with an agent.

"She came in, we talked a little while, and then she said she wanted a 7 percent commission. I was flabbergasted. I knew that other agents in the area were charging only 5 percent. She was 2 percent higher. When I began to protest, she wiggled her finger at me and said, 'You've got a miserable little house in a crime-ridden neighborhood. You should be glad I'm willing to list it at all!'"

There's usually a pause in the story at this point where I'm supposed to ask, "So what did you do?" He's a good friend, so I usually go along.

"Why, I threw her out! I told her I didn't need to sell. We lived there another five years and then I sold it myself for twice what we paid! Now that's getting a good deal."

I suppose this story is supposed to have several morals, one of which is that agents are greedy know-nothings and another is that my friend is a real wheeler and dealer. The truth of the matter, however, is that I knew him when he lived in that house and it indeed was small, miserable, and in a terrible neighborhood. I can understand why an agent would want a bigger commission to sell it.

Further, because he didn't list, he had to live there another five years until all real estate took a big hike in price and any fool could have gotten twice the purchase price of five years earlier.

My own moral here is that negotiating the real estate commission with the agent doesn't necessarily mean you will want to lower it. You may want to raise it to get a quicker sale!

TRAP

Beware of any agent who says that the "fixed" or "standard" or "regular" commission is a given amount. In all parts of the country, the rate of commission paid to a licensed agent to list your house is entirely negotiable between you and the agent. There is no set rate. It's whatever the two of you agree upon.

Will You Get What You Pay For?

At the onset, it's important to keep track of what you want out of listing your house with an agent. While, of course, you want to pay as little as you can, on the other hand you also want to sell your property as soon as possible. It's sort of like watching the donut and not the hole. What's really important is selling the property. The agent's fee is, or should be, subordinate to that, not the other way around.

Therefore, when you sit down with an agent to negotiate the fee, you should also be negotiating the service. One is dependent on the other. If you want a lower fee, then perhaps you'll have to expect lesser service. On the other hand, if you get super service, you may need to pay a higher fee. You usually get what you pay for.

How Does the Agent See It?

I think it's important to understand how agents see things. You might say this falls under the category of being informed and questioning authority. If you don't know what the agent has to do to sell your house, you can't really talk price with him or her. You may have unrealistic expectations.

Real estate agents, despite what most people think, on average are not highly paid. Most agents make less than $45,000 a year, even active ones. (Of course, there are always some who make a million, but that really is more the exception than the rule.)

Most active agents (as opposed to those who are part-timers and don't really do much in the field) spend 50 or 60 hours a week, including nights and weekends, at work. They answer calls at all hours, often from their homes. They drive people whom they've often just met into all sorts of neighborhoods. And even when they finish the job and get a sale, they may be threatened with a lawsuit by an angry buyer or seller for something they (or, chances are, someone else) overlooked.

Further, they must pay for their own clothes (agents have to dress well); their car, including gas, maintenance, and insurance; and sometimes even their own office space and advertising. And on most deals they finally make, they must split the commission between a listing and selling office. If the agent is only a salesperson, the commission must be further split between the salesperson and the broker. (And there's no salary—no deal, no income.)

No, I'm not an apologist for agents, though I may sound like one here. It's just that I've been there and I know what it's like. To simply say that an agent, a good one, doesn't earn his or her commission is poppycock. To a seller, the agent's work and expenses may not always be obvious. But rest assured, a lot of work and expense go into selling properties.

How Does the Buyer See It?

I'm sure you're familiar with this situation. You've got a house worth $400,000. You want to sell it, and an agent waltzes in and asks for a 6 percent commission, a full $24,000. Chances are you owe $300,000 on the house, so the agent is asking for nearly a quarter of your $100,000 equity just to find a buyer! (If you owe more, the agent's percentage of your equity is going to be even higher.)

Further, the house just down the street sold for full price within two days of being listed. Just how much effort did that take on the part of the agent? It's unconscionable, you say.

However, what are your choices? You could always sell the property yourself if you have the time, the patience, and the know-how.

Most people simply don't want to do that. (Those who do are often amply rewarded. See Chapter 12.) The fact is that about 85 to 90 percent of all residential real estate in most areas is sold through agents. When buyers want to see properties, they contact an agent. When sellers want to sell, they list with an agent.

So, as a seller, it now becomes a matter of negotiating the agent's fee downward. The agent wants 6 percent; you want to pay 1 percent. The agent wants to get a full commission because of his or her expenses, time, and so on. Your hope is to get the fee knocked down so you won't be "throwing away" so much of your equity. The result, of course, is negotiation.

TRAP

When you're negotiating with an agent, remember that the agent's choices are limited too. The agent has a choice of listing your property at whatever rate he or she can get or walking away. If the agent walks, time spent on you is wasted for him or her. Some agents, therefore, will ultimately accept any commission rate and then do nothing to sell the property. Their rationale is the following: If by chance it sells, they get something. If it doesn't, they haven't invested any more of their time. You want to avoid this sort of arrangement like the plague.

How Does the Commission Impact the Agent's Role in Selling?

What does an agent do for you? A good active real estate agent who makes a concerted effort to sell your property will do the following. Besides the obvious sales tools such as placing advertising in newspapers, holding open houses, putting a sign on the property, and installing a "lockbox" so other agents can show it, your broker will also "talk up" your house at sales meetings. Large brokerage firms have at least one sales meeting a week, which all agents attend. If your agent "co-brokers" the property (shares the listing with other brokers and, accordingly, splits the commission), he or she should attend MLS (multiple listing services) meetings at least twice a month. Here, agents from all the real estate companies in the area meet. Your agent can stand up at these meetings and tell other agents from dozens of other offices about this wonderful property (yours) she has listed—its features, low price, good terms, and so on. If your agent attends enough of these meetings, talks up your property to enough other agents (and follows through with phone calls and e-mails), chances are he or she will find one of them who is working with the buyer who could be just right for your property.

TRAP

 Some agents won't want to co-broker your home. They'll tell you they have a better chance of selling if they only list for their office. (They'll advertise it more, show it more, and so on.) This is nonsense. You want the maximum number of agents made aware of and working on your house. If a broker insists on not co-brokering a property, I'd wonder if he or she was just trying to avoid splitting a commission.

In other words, the most effective thing your agent can do is "talk up" your house to as many other agents as possible. Since agents in the area are in contact with the vast majority of buyers, this immediately increases your chances that the right buyer will hear about your home.

On the other hand, let's say you negotiate a reduced commission. Now, your agent stands up before other agents at a large sales meeting and describes how well your four-bedroom, three-bath house shows to buyers. A colleague raises a hand and asks, "What's the commission rate?"

Your agent replies, "Four percent."

If there are a lot of houses listed at 5, 6, and even 7 percent, whose houses do you think agents are inclined to show their clients first?

TIP

 Buyers' agents are required to show buyers all properties that are appropriate for them, without regard to what commission rate they might make. That's part of their fiduciary relationship to the buyer. In the real world, however, where judgment is a big factor, that's not the way things always work out.

On the other hand, let's say that you have negotiated something quite different. You have told your agent you're willing to pay a 3 percent commission to the agent who brings in a buyer. That's half of what happens to be a commonly paid commission in your area at the time.

When your agent stands up and is asked what the commission is, he or she can truthfully say, "It's a full 3 percent to the buyer's agent." Now your house is marketable.

Adding a Bonus

Further, you say you're offering an all-expense-paid week in Hawaii to the agent who brings in a buyer. Now, your agent stands up at one of these crucial meetings and describes your house. When someone asks what the commission rate is, your broker beams and says, "My client will not only pay a full 3 percent buyer's agent's commission, she will also give an all-expense-paid week in Hawaii to the buyer's agent!" You should be able to hear the cheers.

Now, when another agent has a prospective buyer and has the choice of showing them your house or someone else's, where do you think the buyer will be steered?

TIP

Rather than increasing the rate of the commission, offer bonuses to agents who sell quickly or who sell at all. Trips, television sets, even an old car or boat that you own and want to get rid of can be offered. So long as the item is tangible (not money), it has the potential of capturing the imagination of other agents and helps to make your property stand out. Also, most such bonuses are actually cheaper than offering a higher commission.

What About Only Giving the Selling Agent—Your Agent— a Lower Commission?

When you negotiate with an agent over a commission, what should be most important in your mind is the service the agent is going to perform. You should talk about how the agent is going to promote your home. You should be concerned with:

Will the agent "talk up" your home at sales meetings? How many? How often? To how many agents?

Will your agent co-broker the property with other agents in the area? Will he or she list your property on the multiple listing service?

What plusses can the agent find to help induce other agents to bring buyers to your house?

How much advertising will the listing agency do as a whole? It's necessary to do more than just advertise your specific home to find a buyer for it. Large amounts of advertising bring in lots of buyers, one of whom may be just right.

Does your agent have other sources of potential buyers? For example, does the listing office have contacts with other offices nationwide that might refer transferees to your area?

In other words, what you should really be negotiating about is what the agent will do to promote the sale of your property, especially how he or she will talk it up to other agents. Only when you've reached a satisfactory arrangement for services should you negotiate price.

Should You Tie the Fee to the Services Performed?

All agents will (or should) tell you up front that the listing fee is negotiable. However, they may also say something such as, "Even though the fee is negotiable, our office accepts only listings for 6 percent." Or "Our bottom line is no less than 5 percent." The agent can legitimately turn down a listing if he or she feels the commission rate is too low.

On the other hand, you can point out other factors. For example, if the market is strong, it doesn't take a whole lot of effort to sell a home. When buyers are plentiful and frequently bid against one another for each house as it is listed, there's much less work for a commission.

In a situation where properties are selling almost as fast as listed, it's silly to pay a full seller's agent's commission. Since the market is so hot, it won't really make much difference (perhaps a few weeks) whether you offer the agent 3 percent or 1 percent. As soon as a sign goes up, buyers will come by.

Further, in a hot market, listing rates tend to fall. You're not the only one who realizes that paying the full rate is foolish. Other sellers do as well and that puts downward pressure on the market. For example, in some areas of the Northwest, the average commission rates (combined buyer's and seller's agents) are only around 4 percent.

Agents may still try to get a higher listing commission rate, but savvy buyers won't let them. Besides, in such a market, sales are so plentiful that almost any agent should do well regardless of the listing rate.

However, in a very slow market, attempting to cut the commission rate would probably work against you. If you are serious about selling, you will want to get out of your property as quickly as possible, before the value drops further. That means getting as many agents as possible working for you, and a high commission rate can help. I have seen sellers negotiate a 7 percent commission when 6 percent was common, so long as the agent promised quick action on a short-term listing.

TIP

Remember, time is money.

Should You Deal with Discount Brokers?

If you have an agent who won't negotiate downward the selling agent's commission, you have other alternatives. There are agents out there who regularly work for less.

"Assist-2-Sell," "Help-U-Sell," and other national realty agencies have a much lower "standard" rate. Some even offer a sliding scale of commission rates that depends on just how much work you do as part of the selling. If you show the house and pay for the advertising, you might get a 1 percent seller's agent's rate, for example. For just handling the paper work, some brokers will simply charge a flat fee, say $1,000 or $2,000. On the other hand, if you want full service, you might end up paying 3 or more percent to the selling agent.

Does it pay to deal with discount real estate companies?

My own experience is that you get what you pay for. Today, discount brokers list their homes on multiple listing services right along with full-service brokers. Their commission rate is also given on every listing.

As noted, in a hot market it is probably foolish to list for a high rate since your house is likely to sell no matter how much or how little effort is poured into it. In a cold market, however, you need all the help you can get.

What About Negotiating the Commission as a Percentage of Equity?

At various times in the past, I've seen ideas put forth that would change the listing system in real estate. Instead of the listing commission being a percentage of the sale price, it would be a percentage of the equity.

For example, you have a house that sells for $200,000 and you list at a 6 percent commission. The agent receives $12,000.

On the other hand, you have only $40,000 in equity in your property; the rest is mortgaged. If the agent's fees were based on equity, at 6 percent the agent would receive only $2,400.

I know that sellers will be enthusiastic about this sort of arrangement, but any real estate agent I know will explain that it simply won't work. Few agents can afford to work for that kind of commission. Further, your equity really shouldn't be the basis of the commission, they will argue. After all, the price and the mortgageable amount are based not on seller's equity, but on what the house is worth on the open market. Why should commission be different? Besides, buyers' agents are paid a commission based on sales price, not seller's equity. Finally, for any given price, there are bound to be hundreds of sellers, each with a different equity. Thus a commission system based on equity simply would be unworkable.

In short, I wouldn't hold out much hope for a system of commission rates based on equity to be enacted by real estate companies any time soon.

Can You Get the Agent to Accept Paper Instead of Cash?

When you sign a listing, all agents will insist on cash. In fact, they will want it written into the listing agreement that you owe them a cash commission if they produce a buyer "ready, willing, and able" to purchase, even if you back out of the sale! But that doesn't necessarily have to be.

TRAP

The agent is technically entitled to a commission not when the sale closes, but when he or she produces an appropriate buyer. It's something to consider before listing if you're not fully convinced you want to sell. Some sellers will add a clause that the commission is payable only when escrow closes, thus helping to avoid a problem if they decide to pull the home off the market.

TIP

It's not necessary to ask an agent to take cash *or* paper. You could negotiate a split—some cash and the rest paper. There can be any combination of the two, depending on how you negotiate the deal.

Some agents are adamant and will not cut their commissions or accept anything but cash, no matter what. Other agents, however, are willing to compromise on their commission if they see no other way to make this deal and only a remote possibility of other deals occurring on this property.

However, even if your agent is willing to take paper or cut a commission, be aware that other agents are probably involved. If there are two agents involved in the deal, a buyer's agent and a seller's agent, both might have to agree on taking paper or on reducing the commission. Further, you may be dealing with salespeople instead of brokers. Thus, before they can give you the go ahead, they may have to get their broker's permission. And while the salesperson may be eager to make even a reduced commission and a sale, the broker may nix the idea on principle or policy—his or her office simply doesn't do that sort of thing.

All of this is negotiable. The trouble is, when it comes to commissions, you can get so many people involved that the negotiations over the commission can be more extensive and heated than those over the sale!

TIP

If you are going to negotiate the sales commission lower or include paper instead of cash, usually the best time to do this is when you've got a deal in hand and its success or failure hinges on how the commission is handled. It's far harder for the agent to say no then.

The Bottom Line

Keep in mind that sometimes getting the best deal doesn't necessarily mean getting the lowest commission rate. What you want, or should want, is a quick sale and a good price.

8

Negotiating a Sales Agreement

I received a call not long ago from a friend who is now selling real estate after having been laid off from a long career with a high-tech engineering company. He's obviously new to this field and was having trouble with a sale.

"It's falling apart," he said. "I represent the sellers, and we received a good offer from buyers who put up a $10,000 deposit and were paying 10 percent down in cash with a 90 percent loan. Everything seemed 'Go.' The property was scheduled to close last Thursday, then at the last minute, we learned that the lender refused to fund the mortgage. They said there was some problem with the buyers' credit. Apparently the buyers didn't tell us, but they've been shopping around for a loan for over two months and haven't found one yet. What do I do now?"

Looking up, I was going to suggest an appeal to a higher authority, but demurred. Instead, I suggested that my friend find out what the credit problem was by attempting to contact the buyers' agent, the buyers, or the lender and offering aid in any way he could. At the same time, I suggested he immediately put the house back on the market.

My friend said the seller had agreed to a 75-day escrow (very long for a residential sale) and it had 30 days to go. He couldn't very well put the house back on the market yet. "Prayer," I finally suggested aloud. "Try it."

The immediate problem here was that my friend had wobbly (financially speaking) buyers. But the long-term problem was a badly negotiated sales agreement. If my friend had been in real estate longer, he might have demanded a preapproval letter from the buyers before proceeding to the sales agreement. Having that, he could have written into the sales agreement a contingency that the buyers had to produce a firm written letter of commitment from a lender within two weeks that stated that the lender had fully qualified the buyers and was going to fund the purchase.

Although that wouldn't actually guarantee that the lender would fund the money, it would be a strong assurance of that fact. If there was a credit problem, a lender undoubtedly wouldn't have written either letter, the seller would have learned of the credit problem sooner, and either the deal wouldn't have been made or the sellers could have backed out of the deal gracefully, returning the house to the market. This would result in only two weeks of lost selling time, at most.

A second error is that the sellers should have insisted that the time allowed for closing the deal be much shorter, perhaps only 30 days. At the end of that time, the buyers' chance to close would have passed and the sellers could put the house back on the market.

"At least we can keep the deposit," my friend said. (When a buyer loses a deposit it is frequently split between seller and agent.) I told my friend that, sadly, that was very unlikely. Most sales agreements specifically state that if the buyer can't get financing there's no deal, and the deposit is to be returned.

I heard a long "Ohh" on the other end of the line. My friend definitely did not like that answer.

What Should You Look For in a Sales Agreement?

At the onset it's important to understand that the making of a real estate deal does not occur on the sales agreement document. It occurs in the understanding between buyer and seller. The sales agreement should only reflect that understanding. However, the document itself is important because it is the legal record of what the parties had in mind.

TIP

As covered by the Statute of Frauds, all sales agreements for real estate are intended to be legally binding documents and must be in writing.

The key to negotiating a more favorable sales agreement usually lies not in the boilerplate that comes preprinted with the standard form, but in the clauses you add—in other words, the specific terms and conditions (the contingencies) of the sale. Depending on these you can have a better or worse deal and sales agreement. In this chapter, we're going to consider six negotiable areas:

1. Price versus terms
2. The deposit
3. Financing contingency
4. Time
5. Other contingencies
6. Buyer's final approval or walk-through

Our emphasis here will be to help you to understand the consequences of various actions—to gain knowledge so that you'll be better equipped to negotiate the deal that you really want.

TIP

A contingency (or "subject to" statement) is an action that must be performed before the sale can go through. For example, "This sale is subject to my Aunt Hilda's written approval of this property within three days" is a contingency.

Thirty years ago, when I began in real estate, the sales agreement (then called the "Deposit Receipt") was a single-page document with maybe a dozen preprinted lines (referring to such things as "time is the essence of the agreement"). Everything was filled in by the agent, buyer, or seller.

Litigation, however, has made the days of the handwritten sales agreement almost a thing of the past. Too many of the old documents simply didn't stand up in court because of vague or improper language. Today's agreement is quite different, often nearly a dozen pages long, all filled with legal "boilerplate." In some sales agreements there is only room to write in the address, the price, the down payment, and the loan amount. Everything else is preprinted and written by lawyers, including a long list of contingency clauses. If you want one of the clauses to apply, you simply check the box and all parties initial! (Unfortunately, no agreement can anticipate every possible contingency a buyer/seller may want.)

The point, however, is that although buyer and seller may agree to contingencies (or unusual terms and conditions), in order to add these to a modern sales agreement, you may need the services of a lawyer or a very competent real estate agent. Unless you are extremely well versed in real estate, don't attempt to add to or change a real estate sales agreement yourself.

Should You Go For a Better Price or Better Terms?

Some agents think of the sales agreement as having two major parts. The first part is simply the price, the amount to be paid for the property. It occupies only a single line on the document. The second part, however, refers to the terms by which the price will be paid and how title will be given. Virtually all of the remainder of the document comes under this heading.

The two-part breakdown, however, underscores the relationship between price and terms. In any real estate deal, there is usually a trade-off between price and terms. For example, if the buyer is paying all cash within two weeks (or as soon as clear title can be given), you would naturally expect that the price would be lower than if the buyer is putting down no cash, but instead is borrowing money from a lender, the seller, and everyone else. In other words, the worse the terms (usually), the higher the price; the better the terms, the lower the price.

When negotiating the sales agreement (in essence negotiating the deal), therefore, it is valuable to remember the two parts—price and terms. Give on one, get on the other. (This does not mean that you cannot increase the size of the pie or the total package, as noted in earlier chapters. It just means that within the sales agreement, useful division is into the two parts.)

TRAP

Sometimes one party or the other (usually the seller) will get hung up on price. That party becomes convinced that the only way they can get a good deal is to get the desired price. If the other party is savvy, they will go along with the price and, in return, insist on receiving terms that are extremely favorable to themselves. As a result, while one side gets the price they wanted, they may actually be giving up so much in the terms of the deal that they end up losing! Beware of hanging onto price like a lifeboat. It could end up sinking you.

The Deposit

The deposit is a part of the negotiations since it indicates the depth of the buyer's sincerity in making the deal. The buyer is presumably sincere, hence the correct term, *earnest money deposit.* However, there is no reason why a deal cannot be completed without a deposit. But a buyer who does not put up a deposit is suggesting that he or she has little financial commitment to the purchase. A seller is far less inclined to look favorably on an offer without a deposit.

If the deal falls through because of a fault of the buyer (for example, the buyer simply refuses to go forward and buy the property), then presumably the seller is entitled to the deposit. If the deal collapses through no fault of the buyer (for example, the seller can't give clear title), then the buyer is presumably entitled to a full refund.

TRAP

If you're a buyer, be sure that the fact that the deposit is to be used as part of the down payment is specified in any sales agreement you sign, or else the deposit could be interpreted to be in addition to the down payment!

From the seller's perspective, the buyer is presumably putting up money that will be lost if that buyer fails to complete the purchase. It's money at risk. Hence, if the buyer puts up $10,000, it presumably shows that the buyer is quite enthusiastic about the property and committed to the purchase.

Who Gets the Deposit?   Consider Sally, who wants to buy a home and puts up a $5,000 deposit. As soon as the seller, John, accepts the offer, he is entitled to that money. It should be paid directly to him. Later, if the deal doesn't go through due to a fault of John's, then it's up to Sally to get the deposit back from John. However, if John isn't entirely scrupulous or just not very good at handling money, he may not want or be able to pay Sally back. Sally eventually might need to go to court and sue John for the recovery. The trouble is, of course, that the suit could cost more than the amount of the deposit to be recovered!

As you can see, this could be a messy business. It's a poor way to handle a deposit. Further, if an agent were involved, chances are that both Sally and John would blame that poor soul for what happened in the deal and insist that the agent come up with the money.

More than anyone else, agents who are involved with deposits on a day-to-day basis realize the problems and potential pitfalls involved with giving the deposit to the seller. Therefore, most agents suggest that the buyer make the deposit to a third party. One choice is the agent, who can then keep it in a trust account. The trouble with this is that if the agent is the fiduciary of the seller and the seller insists on getting the deposit, the agent could feel obligated to turn it over . . . and then answer to the buyer about where the money went. This puts the agent in an even worse position.

Therefore, today most agents insist that the buyer make the deposit check to an escrow company. If the offer is accepted, the check is immediately deposited into escrow and there it sits until the deal is concluded . . . or later.

The "Or Later" Problem.   If the deal isn't concluded for any reason, that deposit usually continues to sit in the escrow account. The buyer can't get it back unless the seller signs off. The seller can't get it unless the buyer signs off. In actual practice, however, the seller may have difficulty in reselling to someone else with a deposit check from a previous buyer hanging over his head in escrow, so he may sign off simply to be done with the old deal. As a result, the buyer may get the deposit back, sooner or later.

TRAP

Buyer or seller can go to court and sue the other party to get the deposit check released out of escrow. But in residential real estate, the deposits are usually too small to warrant such expensive action. It's simpler to just settle.

TIP

A settlement regarding who gets the deposit when a deal goes sour is negotiable. While most often the buyer gets it all back (real estate agents prefer this because it tends to help their reputations and avoid malpractice lawsuits against them), it doesn't have to be the case. The seller could get it all, or it could be split.

Sometimes a clever buyer will include a clause in the agreement to the effect that if the deal isn't concluded within 120 days, for whatever reason, any money the buyer deposited into escrow automatically reverts back to the buyer. Some sellers will agree to this, thinking that this is a clause whose intent is to encourage the seller to move the deal along, not realizing that what it really means is that all the buyer has to do is procrastinate to get that deposit back. Savvy sellers often will balk at such a contingency.

Failure to Complete the Transaction.   Thus far, our assumption has been that the deposit is all that's at stake. However, if a buyer fails to go through with a deal without having a valid reason for backing out, the seller might take the buyer to court for failure to complete the deal according to the sales agreement and potentially get a settlement and damages.

The Deposit as Liquidated Damages.   This is a real risk for buyers. It is also a particular risk for agents, who usually get thrust into the middle of such angry actions. Therefore, today many agents include in their sales agreements a clause that specifies, that in the event the buyer does not go through with the sale and has no legitimate reason for backing out, the deposit is automatically to be considered liquidated damages. In other words, the seller gets the money, and in many cases cannot sue for additional damages.

As a buyer you have the option of agreeing or not agreeing with this condition. It's something you should consider and discuss with your attorney.

What Is the True Effect of the Deposit?   Realistically, in residential real estate today, the deposit has the same function it always had—to demonstrate how sincere the buyer is. However, what it really means is that the buyer is willing to tie up a set amount of money for a period of time. Any anticipation by the seller that he or she is going to be getting that money any time soon without a sale may be more wishful thinking than anything else.

How Big Should the Deposit Be?   As far as most sellers are concerned, the bigger the deposit, the better. However, after a certain point, additional amounts of money aren't going to tilt anyone's head. Remember, any realistic seller today knows that the chances of ever getting that deposit if the deal sours may be remote.

Further, in today's transactions, there are really two parts to the deal. The first is when the sales agreement is signed all around. The second is when all of the buyer's contingencies have been removed. (These are such things as giving approval to an inspection report or seller's disclosures, which, until done, allow the buyer to withdraw from the deal without penalty.)

Until the contingencies have been removed, the size of the deposit is mostly moot. After all, if the buyer can easily back out, who cares if it's $5,000 or $50,000?

On the other hand, once all of the buyer's contingencies are removed, it's far harder for him or her to back out of the deal without losing the deposit. Thus, the size now becomes very important. Therefore, savvy sellers will often insist that after all contingencies are removed, the buyer *increase* the size of the deposit. This helps assure the seller that the buyer will, indeed, move forward with the purchase.

TRAP

Sometimes a buyer who has a particularly poor offer will submit a very large deposit. The hope is that the seller will focus on the deposit and not on the deal. Very few sellers are so naive today.

The Financing Contingency

As we saw in the opening example, negotiating strict time-limit contingencies on the buyer for obtaining needed financing should help protect the seller. These days sellers are always concerned (with some good reason) about buyers who talk a good deal, but later can't come up with the money.

One clause that buyers should insist upon (as seen in Chapter 1) is that they can back out of the deal without penalty, *if* they cannot secure needed financing. They might want to specify the very term, type, and interest rate of the mortgage that they need.

On the other hand, a wise seller will not want to put the exact interest rate and payment the buyer is to qualify for in the financing contingency. The reason is that interest rates tend to bob around. If the market rate is 5 percent when the agreement is signed, and that's the rate entered, but it jumps to 6 percent by the time the deal is ready to close, the buyer has a way to back out: he or she can no longer get a 5 percent mortgage.

However, a buyer wants to protect himself or herself from having to go through with a purchase for a higher interest rate (and, accordingly, a higher monthly payment) than he or she feels can be comfortably afforded. Therefore, although the seller may not want to lock in the current interest rate in the sales agreement, the buyer may want to lock in an interest rate.

One way to negotiate a win–win situation for both buyer and seller is to put in a maximum interest rate and payment the buyer will accept. For example, say that rates are currently 6 percent. Perhaps the agreement could call for a loan for "not more than 6.5 percent interest." This limits the buyer's risk should rates rise and also gives some assurance to the seller that the buyer isn't going to use a financing contingency to escape from the deal.

To protect the buyer further, he or she may want to insist that the exact term and type of loan should also be written in as a contingency;

for example, the sale is contingent upon the buyer's applying for and obtaining a fixed-rate mortgage for 30 years with payments of no more than $XX per month and an annual interest rate of no more than X percent. If it's an adjustable-rate mortgage (ARM), that fact and the minimum steps, adjustment periods, margins, and so forth should also be included. (For more information on ARMs, I suggest you check into my book, *Tips and Traps When Mortgage Hunting*, McGraw-Hill, 2005.)

Negotiating the Financing Itself.   Frequently, deals are all cash to the seller. The buyer offers a down payment and gets financing for the balance of the purchase price. Sometimes, however, sellers may want to finance their properties themselves. This is especially the case when the homes are paid off and the sellers are retirees. They may like the idea of having the regular income that a mortgage provides, at a higher rate than a savings account or CD.

If a seller is willing and able to handle all or part of the financing, there usually are far fewer problems with qualifying. This means that a seller offering financing may be able to negotiate a better deal in terms of price and other terms from a needy buyer.

Sometimes financing becomes a deal point. The buyer wants the seller to handle the financing. But the seller doesn't want to do that. How can this be negotiated?

There are a variety of solutions. Sometimes the seller can be induced to carry back a second mortgage he or she doesn't want by:

- Getting a higher price on the sale
- Getting a higher interest rate
- Concessions on time or other conditions in the deal

In other words, if you're the buyer who needs to have a reluctant seller carry back a second mortgage, it may be to your advantage to negotiate a higher price or better terms elsewhere. Again, this will produce a win–win situation. You get what you want (seller financing) by finding something the seller wants.

TRAP

A few years ago unscrupulous speculators abused this deal point by pushing it too far. They asked sellers to carry 100 percent of the financing. In other words, they offered nothing down. They would buy "subject to" the existing first mortgage (meaning they didn't assume liability for it) and the seller would give them a second mortgage for the entire balance. To get sellers to agree, the buyers jacked up the price—often beyond market value. Their plan usually was twofold: first to get hold of the property, rent it out, and wait for rapid price appreciation to overtake them and, second, to sell for a profit, having invested next to nothing. Or the more unscrupulous, having gotten control, would rape the property. They would rent it, keep the rental money, and make no payments to the lender (of the first mortgage) or to the seller (who held the second). By the time foreclosure was completed, they often had up to a year of rent that they had pocketed. The person who got hurt was the seller, who was still responsible for the existing first mortgage and who received no payment on the second mortgage. Some sellers simply lost their properties and their equities. Others got their properties back, but at great expense. As a result, many sellers are still wary of financing the sale of their properties.

Dealing with Time

Time can also be a deal point. In Chapter 2, we saw why time was important as a negotiating tool. Now we'll consider a specific application of time in the sales agreement: the date of occupancy.

When—the exact date—the seller turns the home over to the buyer is usually a point of vital interest to both parties. Normally, occupancy is given to the buyer on the date the house transfers title. But there are exceptions. For example, a few years ago I was selling a vacant house, and the buyers, as part of the sales offer, wanted to be in the property within 30 days. The buyers were coming from Central America and their furniture was arriving in about three weeks. They wanted to have a home ready for it. Also, they didn't want the inconvenience and extra expense of renting a motel room.

The problem was that, at the time, the earliest a lender could arrange financing was four weeks, probably closer to five. That meant that the buyer wanted to be in the premises for one to two weeks before the deal could close. The buyer wanted to get possession of my vacant house before the deal closed.

What's the Problem Here? To see the problem, you have to look at the downside risk. What if the buyer moved in, eventually couldn't get financing, and the deal couldn't close? What if the buyer decided to back out of the purchase? In short, there are many scenarios that would lead to the deal's not closing. Also, if I gave possession prior to closing, I'd now have someone in the property, and getting them out later might turn into a big problem. Obviously, timing was a deal point here and a great inconvenience for me. Why should I bother with all the hassle involved? Why not simply dump the deal?

The buyers understood the problem. So they offered me very close to full price and no other conditions—I would receive all cash with most of it coming from their new loan. I would get nearly my full price and all cash, something I wanted and something that was a strong inducement for me to find a way to make it work.

Ultimately, I had the buyers sign a month-to-month rental agreement, putting up both first month's rent plus a substantial security/cleaning deposit outside of escrow (paid directly to me). The sales agreement stipulated, however, that if they bought the property within five weeks (which should be enough time for them to secure financing), all the rental money, including the deposit, became part of the down payment. If they didn't buy, then, of course, they were tenants.

They were satisfied with the deal. They had a house to move into when they needed it. I was likewise satisfied. I had a pretty sure shot at a sale. And if the sale didn't go through, then I had the property rented. Since the house was a rental anyway, this fit in well with my plans. Ultimately, the buyers did qualify, did get the mortgage, and the deal closed—a successful negotiation of time.

TRAP

One of the dangers of letting a buyer in before closing is that, if the deal doesn't close, the buyer then may be considered a tenant with tenant's rights. This means that if the buyer refuses to move or pay rent, you might have to go through expensive and potentially lengthy (if the buyer contests) eviction procedures to remove them from the house.

Of course, this can work both ways. Sometimes a seller wants to stay after the transaction closes. Buyers have to be wary of this, lest they later have difficulty getting the former seller to leave the premises.

And there's also the problem of what condition the property will be in when the seller/buyer finally leaves, even if the transaction closes. There's realistically no opportunity here for the other party to inspect prior to closing if someone is already in the house.

TIP

A different concern with regard to time that we saw in the first example of this chapter is that the property is usually taken off the market once buyers sign a sales agreement. If the house is off the market a month or so while the buyer hunts for a mortgage, and if ultimately the deal falls through, that's a lot of time wasted during which another potential buyer could be found. Some sellers will, therefore, negotiate a clause in the sales agreement that allows them to continue showing the property and to take back-up offers until the deal closes.

As a buyer, the problem here is that if I have trouble securing financing or the closing is delayed for any reason, and the seller has another, better back-up offer, I could lose the deal. Before granting permission for the seller to keep showing the property and to take back-up offers, therefore, a buyer should negotiate a concession elsewhere.

Other Contingencies

I used to know a builder who always said, "I don't care what the sales agreement says, as long as there's a 'subject to' in it." He was, of course, referring to a contingency clause, a condition that said the sale was subject to the occurrence of some action (or lack of action). While I think he was a bit careless in not caring what the clause was about, his point was well taken. Almost any contingency will weaken a sales agreement and threaten it if there's a lawsuit and the matter gets to court.

112

Some buyers, well aware of this, will insist on one or more contingency clauses. This, they feel, gives them a way to back out of the deal and not have a concern over the deposit's being tied up. When the sole purpose of these contingencies is to offer a back door out, I refer to them as frivolous contingencies.

On the other hand, sometimes the buyers are sincere but new to real estate or simply want to have a lot of such clauses inserted because it makes them feel more secure. Knowing they can back out at any time may be what allows the buyers, psychologically, to make the offer.

From the seller's perspective, each new contingency weakens the deal. If I'm a seller and the buyer insists on, for example, making the sale subject to her husband's getting a raise from his employer or a new job in the area or any such thing, I have to ask myself whether I really want to sign the deal. After all, the buyers can control the contingency. They can forget to ask for a raise or look for a new job. In short, they can back out of the deal any time they want and I'm left holding nothing.

What to Do about Contingencies.   There are three ways to negotiate an unwanted contingency in a sales agreement.

The first is to verbally define what it is. For example, if the buyers insist on what the seller sees as a frivolous contingency and you're the seller, explain that a condition that virtually makes the agreement nonbinding on only the buyers won't be acceptable. Then, once everyone understands what a disadvantage this puts the seller under, you, as a seller, can insist the contingency be removed. Or, if you're to accept it, the buyers have to make other concessions.

Second, if you, the seller, want to move forward with a sales agreement with frivolous contingencies, you may want to insist on the right to keep showing the property and accepting back-up offers. One such contingency is when buyers insist on having the right to first sell their old home before they buy yours, as we saw in Chapter 1. They may want a clause inserted that says the purchase of your home is contingent upon the sale of their existing home. In a hot market, few sellers would be tempted to sign such an offer. However, in a slow market, many sellers would. However, if you're a seller and you do sign, it would be wise to include a sentence or two that not only allowed you to keep showing the property and to take back-up offers, but said that if you got a back-up offer, the buyers would have, for example, 48 hours to remove the contingency or would have to back out of the deal.

In other words, yes, you'll hold your house for the buyers while they try to sell their old home. But, no, you won't take your home off the market. And, if you got a more solid offer, they'd have to agree to buy your home, even without the sale of their home. It's a way to have your cake and eat it too.

Third, smart negotiators will put a time limitation on every contingency. It might be a month or a week or 72 hours, but the buyers (or sellers) would have only a certain amount of time to act on the contingency, or else it would have to be removed. For example, the buyer may want a contingency relating to a home inspection. This is perfectly natural and to be expected. However, the seller may go along only if the buyer agrees to remove the contingency within 14 days. This means the buyer must get the inspection report and approve it within two weeks and sign a release of the contingency. If the buyer fails to do this, then the sale is off and the seller can resell.

Or a purely frivolous contingency may actually be that the buyers want to make the deal subject to the approval of their aunt in Maryland. Maybe they rely heavily on this person's judgment (and financial support!). If everything else in the deal were to my liking and the prospect of another buyer any time soon was slim, yes, I would agree. But, I would put in a time contingency. Yes, you can secure the approval of Aunt Mary, but she has to give it within three days. In other words, the buyers have to remove the contingency within 72 hours to keep the deal alive. But, they may argue, it will take longer than that for Aunt Mary to get out here to see the house. Fine, make it four days.

The point is that almost any kind of frivolous contingency can be mitigated by stipulating a strict time limit. It has to be cleared within certain time parameters for the deal to continue. If it isn't cleared, there is no deal.

TIP

Remember, any time you, the buyer, offer a contingency, particularly a frivolous one, you are making a weaker offer and will undoubtedly have to pay for it either by having the offer rejected outright, or by making concessions in price or other terms. A savvy buyer will put in as *few* contingencies as possible to get better terms and price.

TRAP

I've seen some gutsy buyers in a hot market pull the financing contingency out! They knew they were competing with other buyers for the same property and they made a totally "noncontingent" offer. They would buy the property, period. I've even seen such buyers make the deposit check out directly to the seller! What this means, of course, is that if they can't conclude the sale for any reason, they are likely to lose their deposit. And, they could have an angry seller pursuing them in litigation. I don't suggest such an offer for the faint of heart.

The Final Walk-Through

Most sales agreements today provide for a final walk-through by the buyer, usually the day before the deal closes (when title transfers, the seller gets the money, and the buyer gets the house). The reason this walk-through came about, as have so many other things in real estate, is largely to protect agents.

In the past, buyers would not see the property, at least the inside, between the time they first made the offer and the time they finally got clear title. However, during that period the seller might have had orgies every night. The walls might be stained with food, the floors awash in wine, the toilet fixtures ripped out . . . No, it's not likely. But, believe it or not, I have seen this sort of thing happen!

When the buyers take possession, bright-eyed and anticipating a lovely new home, they are aghast at what they find. And whom do they blame? The agent, of course—but also the seller. In the past, agents have had to pay to make up for the actions of irresponsible sellers. And sellers have lost deals because of their carelessness or negligence.

Therefore, to help prevent any of this from happening, the "final walk-through" came into popularity. Here, the buyer is allowed to see the property just before the deal closes to be sure that it's just as it was when the offer was made.

The walk-through also has the effect of putting the sellers on notice that they had better keep the home shipshape, because it will have to pass inspection before the deal can close. The actual result of all this, however, is that agents don't have to deal with angry buyers and partying sellers.

The purpose of the final walk-through, therefore, is to make sure the physical condition of the property hasn't changed, and that's what's usually specified in the contract clause that describes it. However, sometimes buyers see this as a last-minute opportunity to negotiate their way out of the deal.

I have some friends who were buying a townhouse near Los Angeles. (A townhouse normally only has common walls connecting with another home—there is land beneath and sky above.) It was a nice property and they qualified for the financing. Eventually all the contingencies, except the walk-through, were removed. However, just before the sale was to close, they discovered another townhouse nearby that was bigger, cost less, and was in a better neighborhood. Naturally they wanted out of the deal they had made so they could buy the other townhouse. However, their reasons for wanting out were not likely to appeal to the seller of the first property.

So they confronted their agent and explained their dilemma. The agent said she would "fix it," and she did.

The agent led them through their final walk-through and suggested that perhaps things weren't as they had originally been. They agreed. The agent then presented a huge list of problems with the property to the seller, problems that would have cost a fortune to fix. The seller, naturally, said that obviously the buyers were trying to back out. The property hadn't deteriorated that much since the offer was made. The agent simply said, "Maybe." Then she emphasized that the buyers were exercising their right under the final walk-through contingency. Ultimately they just did not find the property suitable.

In this true story, the seller finally said okay and released the buyers, signing off and returning the deposit. The agent then sold my friends the other townhouse and completed the deal.

What Could the Sellers Have Done?   The sellers could have insisted that the buyers complete the sale. The sellers could have demanded the deposit. The trouble was that there was the matter of that final walk-through contingency. The way it had been written, it gave the buyers the power to reject the property right up until the last minute.

What the sellers could have done is negotiate for a tougher walk-through contingency. They could have had an attorney check the final walk-through contingency clause. The wording could have been strengthened so that there was less chance the buyers could use it as a way to back out of the deal.

9

Offer and Counteroffer

In the vast majority of real estate transactions, the buyers and sellers don't negotiate with each other. Rather, each has an agent, and the negotiations are carried on through those agents. In this chapter we'll see how to negotiate through offer and counteroffer when the agent is the intermediary.

Negotiating through an agent has pros and cons. On the plus side, you can vent your feelings to the agent about the house and seller and not worry about offending the seller. You can openly complain that the seller is a miserable housekeeper and you wouldn't keep a dog in a place in that condition. The agent will never mention it to the seller.

On the minus side, all the information that you get about the other party comes from the agent. If your broker isn't perceptive or forthright, you could get a skewed perspective about the seller that could lead you to accept an offer for too little or to counter for too much.

117

example, a seller's agent can't reveal that the seller has said, "I'd be willing to sell for $10,000 less than I'm asking," unless the seller authorizes the agent to say this. Similarly, a buyer's agent can't reveal to the seller the buyer's top price for the property unless authorized. Further, if you're a buyer working with a seller's agent and you tell that agent that although you're making an offer for one price, you'd actually be willing to pay $10,000 more, the agent is ethically bound to reveal that information to the seller! The same holds true in reverse for a buyer's agent.

Therefore, as a buyer, you frequently need to use your best negotiating tactics both on the seller and the agent. This means that you will want to hold your cards fairly close to your vest.

Yes, ask the agent for opinions both on the true value of the property and on the amount to offer. Yes, consider carefully what the agent says and then ask the agent what he or she would do in your situation. But always take a moment to come away and weigh what has been said against the scale of competence, the fiduciary responsibilities of the agent (briefly described in the Trap above), and common sense. Ultimately, you need to make your own decision.

TIP

In a real estate transaction, the only person you can count on to be 100 percent on your side is you.

The Procedure for Offers

When you're dealing through an agent, offers and counteroffers are presented in written form. You make an offer and the agent, in consultation, writes it out on a sales agreement. Then the agent presents the offer to the other party and, presumably, argues your case for you.

If the offer is accepted, fine. You've got a deal. However, I suspect that in better than 70 percent of the cases, the buyer's original offer is not accepted, but instead the seller counteroffers. The agent will then come back and explain the seller's position, may even argue for accepting the seller's counteroffer, or may make suggestions about countering the counter.

Offer and Counteroffer

1. The buyer makes an offer that the agent writes up. The offer usually has a time limit for acceptance.

2. As soon as possible, the agent presents the offer to the seller.

3. The seller accepts the offer exactly as written up, or rejects it. An offer that's rejected is effectively dead. A counter does not resurrect a dead offer—it's actually a new offer.

4. If the seller rejects the offer, the seller may choose to counter. The counter will presumably be for less than the seller originally wanted, but more than the buyer offered. Usually the counter also has a time limit for acceptance.

TIP

Remember the concept of a package. The counter may, for example, maintain the seller's original price, but offer better terms or time. (It is possible for the seller to counter with exactly the originally desired price and terms—a "take it or leave it" counter.)

5. The buyer may now accept or reject the seller's offer. The buyer, however, is under no obligation to accept any counteroffer from the seller.

6. If the buyer rejects the seller's counter, he or she may choose to make another counteroffer.

7. The offering and counteroffering can continue almost indefinitely. There are no limits to the number of times the negotiations can go back and forth.

TIP

Remember, the agent is now negotiating for you. If the agent is skilled and determined, you have a much better chance of getting any offer accepted. That's why it's important to pick agents at the onset whom you believe are good negotiators, not just friendly faces.

TRAP

If you're going to counter, it's usually a good idea to make the counter on the same document as the original offer. The reason is psychological. When the counter is on the same document, even though the other party knows that his or her original offer was rejected, it makes it seem like the same deal is still being negotiated. The same holds true for counter-counters. Better to wear out the paper on a sales agreement than lose the deal.

Why Would a Buyer Want a Counteroffer?

In Chapter 6, we discussed how much to offer for a property. We were talking about making a serious offer that the seller would accept. In a great many instances where a deal is actually made, the seller's counter contains only minor changes. However, sometimes as a buyer you may not really expect the seller to accept your offer. Indeed, you may make a "lowball" offer that's so far below the asking price or contains such inferior terms that you know no reasonable seller will accept it. Why would a buyer make such an offer to a seller?

The reason is that the buyer may want a counteroffer back from the seller. There are many reasons for wanting a counteroffer including:

Reasons for Wanting a Counteroffer

1. The seller has an unrealistically high asking price. By making an unrealistically low offer, you, the buyer, hope to compromise somewhere in between.

2. You simply can't afford anywhere near what the seller is asking. So you offer something close to your maximum, hoping the seller will be desperate enough to counter near your offer.

3. You simply want to "steal" the property. When the seller counters, you'll again offer close to your initial low price, hoping that by now the seller will be discouraged enough to accept.

4. You simply want to get the negotiations opened. Once offers are flying through the air, you hope to learn enough about the seller to determine the best price you can get.

Why Would a Seller Want to Counter?

As a seller represented by an agent, you probably don't have much of a handle on what kind of a person the buyer is. (That's the reason I sometimes recommend face-to-face negotiations.) Rather, you have to judge partly by what the agent reports, but mainly by what the buyer does. You have to watch the buyer's actions, and these are in the form of an offer.

Not long ago a friend of mine was selling a house that was in dire straits. The house was on a steep hillside and built on an old streambed. During the rainy season, that stream came back to life, and over the years it had eroded much of the foundation of my friend's home. The house now teetered precariously on what was left of the foundation. My friend knew that his only chance of selling was to find a buyer who would be willing to take the property "as is" and fix it.

TRAP

Any time you see a house advertised "as is," you can figure it has big problems. Although some agents advise all sellers to sell "as is" as a way of protecting themselves against buyers' later coming back with a lawsuit claiming some defect wasn't disclosed, I don't believe such a course of action will work. Whether a house is sold "as is" or not, the seller still has to disclose all defects to the buyer. All that happens when a seller tries to sell "as is"

is that you're put on notice that there's something seriously wrong with the property. As a result, you'll probably want to offer much less for it.

TIP

If you're a seller, it's usually better, in my opinion, not
to sell "as is." Just disclose all problems and if there's
something in particular that you don't want to warrant,
make sure the buyers sign off as being aware of that
particular defect when they accept the property.

Therefore, when my friend got a purchase offer for a ridiculously
low price, he countered by including a paragraph in the sales agreement that said the buyer was fully aware of the foundation problems
and accepted them. He also asked a higher price.

The first two buyers that offered were scared away by the counter.
They had hoped (without much reason) that the seller would either
sell for just the value of the land or fix the problem as part of the sale.

The third buyer, however, had experience in building construction and was fascinated by the challenge posed by my friend's house.
He accepted the paragraph regarding the foundation problems and
proceeded to negotiate a price that he felt would be justified given
the condition of the property. My friend, the seller, had achieved his
objective of finding a buyer who could handle the problem and
would not want so low a price as to be buying the land only.
Ultimately, after going back and forth many times, a deal was signed.

The Three Types of Offers

Buyers can make three kinds of offers:

1. *Lowball.*   The offer is ridiculously below what the seller is asking. The hope is that the seller will counter at a compromise
   price.

2. *"Close to asking."*   The buyer simply wants the property and is willing to pay the seller's price. However, the buyer is hoping the
   seller will come down a little rather than chancing that the seller

will simply reject the bid or counter.

3. *Compromise.* The offer is somewhere in between, because the buyer is looking for a series of counters.

The Two Types of Counters

The seller has only two realistic choices in a counteroffer:

1. *Highball.* The seller rejects the buyer's offer and comes back almost to the asking price. The seller's motivation here is simply to keep the negotiations open in the hope that the buyer will eventually "come around."

2. *Compromise.* The seller counters with somewhere in between the asking price and the buyer's offer. The seller is hoping that negotiations will eventually result in an acceptable price.

TIP

To my mind, there's little point in the seller's countering a buyer's "close to asking" offer. Better to simply accept it than run the risk that the buyer will simply walk away in a huff. On the other hand, some hardnosed sellers will simply counter such an offer by writing in the exact asking price and terms. Sometimes they win and get a deal. But sometimes the buyer gets offended and walks.

Beware of an agent who comes back after presenting your offer (or counteroffer) and says something like, "We have a deal, congratulations. Oh, by the way, the other party made a few minor changes and I'll come by and have you initial them." That's incorrect. Any changes at all mean the offer (or counter) was rejected. You now no longer have any obligation to the deal. When the agent comes by for countersigning, what's really being presented to you is a totally new counteroffer.

The Bottom Line

My best advice in offering and counteroffering is, "Always strive to keep the negotiations open until you succeed, or simply give up." I've countered what I thought were hopeless offers only to have the other party rethink its position and come back with something more realistic.

10

Leverage the Inspection Report

Recently I received a letter from a couple who had purchased an earlier *Tips and Traps* book in which I mentioned that when buying a home, it is possible to use an inspection report to get a better price. They reported they had done this and had gotten a price reduction of $31,500 on a $212,000 price. They explained that they had made an offer on a home in a mountainous area. They had gotten the best deal they could and had included a contingency that the transaction was subject to their approving a home inspection.

The couple hired a retired engineer to give the inspection, and he had concluded that the house had a bad foundation. Parts of it were cracked and some serious repair work had to be done. In addition, because of this, several perimeter wall areas were sagging and needed to be fixed. Armed with the report, the buyers had leveraged the seller into reducing his price by nearly 15 percent. They had purchased the property, and they had been able to get the repair work done for a fraction of the estimated cost. Needless to say, they were thrilled with the deal.

How Leveraging the Inspection Report Works

It's important to understand that today virtually all home transfers include a professional home inspection. As noted earlier, the reason for this is twofold. The first and most obvious reason is that buyers want a better handle on what they are purchasing. Most purchasers simply do not have the knowledge to determine the condition of a property. Therefore, they are willing to pay an inspector to take a look and give them a report. The second reason is to negotiate a better deal.

TIP

The inspection report is often made after the deal is signed. This means that when negotiations take place, typically, the true condition of the property may be unknown.

Therefore, savvy buyers make the deal contingent upon their approving the inspection report. If the report comes back negative, they can back out of the deal with no harm to themselves. Sellers, as noted in Chapter 3, can help protect themselves by putting a time limit on the buyer's approval. The buyer has 7 or 10 or however many days to approve the report, or else the deal is gone and the seller can accept other offers.

The inspection report, thus, becomes a valuable discovery tool for both buyer and seller. It also can be a vital negotiating tool. But to see how, we must first remember that the value of a home is determined to a large extent by the condition of the physical structure itself. (The lot and location are the other parts of the value.) Therefore, when you buy a home, the price you're paying includes, presumably, a house in good shape (except for problems as disclosed by the seller).

In fact, when you, as a buyer, make an offer and negotiate a sale, you assume the house is okay except for whatever defects the seller discloses. Defects, which can be problems as severe as foundation cracks or as minor as chipping paint, change what you are buying and, hence, affect the price you are (or should be) willing to pay.

TIP

In most states today, a seller's disclosure statement is given at or near the time the sales agreement is signed. In California, for example, the seller gives the buyer a disclosure statement (describing all defects in the property) upon signing the sales agreement. The reason is that in California the buyer usually has three days after receiving the disclosure in which to back out of the deal with no penalty. The sooner the buyer receives the disclosure, the sooner the backing out period ends.

How to Leverage during Negotiations

There are two occasions when an inspection report can leverage a better deal. The first is when the deal is originally negotiated. Usually this happens when the seller has previously had the house inspected.

If the seller has an existing inspection report, it may reveal defects or problems. As a buyer, you may point these out and use them as arguments to leverage a lower price. On the other hand, however, the seller may already have taken this into account and may be asking a lower price. As a buyer, you may feel more off the price is justified.

On the other hand, a seller can also use an inspection report as leverage. For example, the seller may point out that based on an existing inspection report, which revealed few or no problems, the buyer shouldn't hesitate to offer more for the property. In a sense, the buyer already has assurances of the soundness of the home. (A savvy buyer, as noted above, will still insist on his or her own report, with a contingency referring to it in the sales agreement.)

TIP

A seller with an existing inspection report can balk at having a buyer get a new inspection with some justification, saying it will just slow down the deal. Further, if the buyer insists on an inspection contingency, the seller with an existing report may insist it's a deal point and ask for concessions elsewhere. Nevertheless, these reports have become so common that in most instances the seller simply accepts their necessity.

Renegotiating

The second occasion when an inspection can be used to leverage a better deal is after the report has been made. It's at this point that negotiations may actually be reopened.

Sally and Ted were buying a home that the seller represented to them as being in "perfect condition." It certainly looked sharp, with beautiful landscaping in front, a new paint job, and a pleasing rustic backyard. But they insisted on a professional inspection and made the deal contingent upon their approving it. The seller said, "Sure." After all, the seller felt the property was terrific.

Sally and Ted hired a person who had previously been a building inspector to conduct the inspection for them. He had been around construction all his life and, because of his experience in his previous profession, claimed to know just what to look for.

The inspection took about four hours, probably twice as long as most, and revealed a whole laundry list of problems, some minor, some more severe. For example, the gas forced-air furnace had a hole in the heat exchanger. It would probably have to be replaced. The plumbing under the sink in one bathroom was nearly rotted out and also would have to be replaced. Worse, the chimney had cracked and would need to be rebuilt. But, worst of all, the roof, though it appeared fine from the ground, was wood shingle, and many shingles were missing. The inspector pointed out there were many cracks and holes that could be seen when looking up from underneath in the attic. He recommended having the roof replaced.

The seller was aghast at the report and, quite frankly, so were Sally and Ted. They had thought they were buying a home in great condition. Now it turned out that the house had severe problems. Sally and Ted said they wanted to get a handle on how much cost was involved, and they hired several contractors to come in and quickly give them bids on repair and replacement work. The total was in excess of $48,000.

Now Sally and Ted went back to the negotiating table. They said they wanted the work done and the seller to pay for it. The seller stubbornly refused. He said it was too much money. He simply wouldn't do it. Let them back out of the deal. He'd sell it to someone else.

Sally pointed out that in any future deals the seller would have to reveal the current inspection report, and any other buyer would be just as likely to want the work done. Further, Ted casually mentioned that if the seller hid the report, he was opening himself up for a tremendous lawsuit from a new buyer. The seller decided to rethink his position. Eventually, the seller had the chimney, furnace, and plumbing fixed (for substantially less than Sally and Ted's original estimates). And he gave them $10,000 off the price for the bad roof.

Once the deal went through and Sally and Ted moved in, Ted got several flats of shingles, went out on the roof, and over a weekend made repairs himself. The total cost was under $500. Of course, it was not a new roof and would eventually need to be replaced. But it would be usable for several more years without leaking. Two years later they resold the property and revealed that the existing roof was old and weathered, but that it did not leak. An inspection subsequently showed that there were no shingles missing and no light coming through cracks visible from below (thanks to Ted's efforts). The next buyer bought the property without quibbling over the roof.

The important point here is that the inspection report required the negotiations to reopen. The report allowed the buyers to convince the seller to lower the price. The inspection report thus became a vital tool for the buyer in leveraging price.

Preinspected Homes

As noted above, sometimes sellers will have an inspection prior to finding a buyer. They may even advertise, "Home is preinspected."

Often this happens when there is a deal that falls through and a would-be buyer paid to have an inspection. The seller now has a copy of that report and makes it available to the next would-be buyer. (Normally, the seller should make all such reports available.) The seller usually hopes the buyer will accept this report and sign off on a deal without contingencies.

The problem here is that if you're the buyer, you really don't know under what circumstances the previous report was made. Did the inspector do a competent job? Did the previous would-be buyer go along and ask questions and point out potential problems? (Often the verbal explanations of a home inspector are the most revealing and helpful part of the process.) Was the inspector a relative of the seller?

Therefore, I always suggest that you have your own inspection done (and pay for it—usually around $350) along with a contingency pertaining to it. Yes, accept a previous report and read it with a grain of salt. But, until your own inspector is out there, and you along with him, you really don't feel that you have a true handle on the property's condition.

Why Would Sellers Want a Home Inspection?

A not so obvious reason for a home inspection is that sellers also want it. This is largely due to the fact that we live in a litigious society, and buyers have successfully sued sellers for either damages or rescission (when the deal is rescinded and the seller has to return the buyer's money and take back the property) because of undisclosed defects. With a formal inspection, however, the seller can point out that every effort was made to reveal the true condition of the property and, therefore, the purchaser has less recourse if a problem is later discovered. (Agents likewise love inspections because without them the broker is frequently the one blamed when the buyer discovers a defect.)

Dealing with Lenders

There are important financing considerations that need to be taken into account whenever the price is lowered after the sales agreement has been signed because of a professional inspection. Basically, they revolve around the fact that lenders do not want to make loans on properties that need repair work. In order to get the financing, the work normally has to be completed first. For example, the inspection report may say that the chimney has to be rebuilt. If the buyer and seller now sign an addendum to the sales agreement saying that the seller will have the chimney rebuilt, the lender will normally want proof of the work having been done before the loan can be funded. This will be a contingency the lender will add to the loan.

On the other hand, if the addendum says that the seller will pay $8,000 back to the buyer (or give the buyer credit for that amount) to compensate for the work that needs to be done on the chimney, the lender may not fund at all, again insisting that the work be done before the deal is concluded and escrow closes.

In other words, any time the sales agreement reflects a repair to the property, the lender will usually insist the repair be done before the deal is concluded. This could preclude a reduction in sales price as compensation for a broken or damaged part of the house.

TIP

Many times the cost of the repair work is variable. Two contractors may have widely differing bids. And if the owners do the work themselves, the cost may be only that of building materials. This is one good reason the seller may want to seriously consider doing work in lieu of reducing price.

TRAP

Whether work reported as necessary on an inspection report needs to be done or not is often a matter of opinion. The buyer may say, "Yes." The seller, "No." In such cases as these (like the roof noted above), it is sometimes preferable to reduce the sales price of the property without reference to the specific reason. In other words, having looked at the inspection report, buyer and seller have renegotiated and determined the original price was too high. As a consequence, they have set it lower. The sale no longer is contingent upon the roof being repaired. In some cases this will satisfy a lender.

Buyers Who "Set Up" Sellers

Buyers can "set up" sellers, although it is not principled and if the seller finds out about it, can cause the deal to be lost or make the negotiations much more difficult. As a seller you should try to be aware of these "set ups."

Joan found a home she wanted to buy. It was owned free and clear by two elderly people who were planning to move into a much smaller condo. Joan gave the house a thorough inspection on her own. Since she had a degree in architecture, she had an excellent feel for what might be wrong with a property. She detected a serious problem. During Joan's inspection, she noted that the house followed the steep slope of the hill on one side. In other words, the house on the west side, where the hill fell away, was actually lower than on the east side. This had resulted in some subtle stress cracks in the foundation and quite a few small cracks on the walls inside. However, the elderly sellers had lived there for years and, as a result, had never noticed the gradual changes of the property. They felt the relatively minor cracks in the interior walls were due to "natural settling." Their real estate agent didn't realize there was a problem either.

Joan made an offer. But instead of bringing her concerns into the open, she negotiated the best price as if the house had no defects. She did, however, insist on a professional home inspection and made the deal contingent upon her approving the report. The sellers, feeling all was well, congratulated themselves on a sale and turned around and bought a condo they had been eyeing.

Joan hired a structural engineer to inspect the property, and he quickly discovered the defect and noted it in the inspection report. Then Joan called out the most expensive construction company in the area to give a bid on repairs. Finally, armed with the report and the bid, she called on the sellers.

Joan's bid for repairs was fully a third of the sales price! The sellers were shocked. But the professional inspection report had been conducted by a highly reputable inspector, as their own agent noted. And the construction company that gave the bid was one of the best in the area. So they felt they could not reasonably challenge the report or the costs of repair.

Further, by now the sellers had committed to purchasing another home. If they were to back out of Joan's deal, they would lose the smaller retirement condo they wanted. Finally, they felt that no matter who bought their house, they would have to reduce the price substantially. (The alternative of having the work done themselves was simply too overwhelming for them.) In the end, they agreed to a one-third price reduction.

Joan quickly bought the property and moved in. She's still living there and hasn't done any repair work. After all, there was nothing dangerous about the condition. She has patted herself on the back many times about her shrewd investment. As for the sellers, they were out a considerable amount of money that they had counted on using for their retirement.

The "Above Board" Approach

On the other hand, Joan might have noted the problem with the house at the time she made her offer. Indeed, she might have made a lower offer initially because of it.

As a result, the sellers would have been made aware and might have hired their own inspector to check it out. Further, they might have gotten bids from several contractors that could have been significantly lower than the bid Joan got. And because this would have been done during the initial negotiations, they wouldn't have committed to buy another house and would have felt free to turn Joan down if her offer was too low. In short, if Joan had been strictly straightforward, she probably would never have been able to leverage the price as low as she had based on the inspection report.

All of this makes it sound as though Joan was a shrewd buyer. However, I do not personally approve of her approach and do not advocate or condone it. Further, I strongly believe, "What goes around comes around." In my own life, I've witnessed a certain symmetry, justice, balance, or whatever you might want to call it, to the universe. If you cheat someone, in my experience, that will come back to haunt you.

In Joan's case (obviously not her real name), this did happen. I saw her nearly 10 years later when she was trying to resell the property. However, by then the erosion on the side of the house with the steep slope had accelerated, and much of the foundation had severely cracked. There was no mistaking to anyone who looked that there was a severe problem here. Indeed, the real estate agent, seeking to protect himself from any liability, called in a city inspector who promptly condemned the house!

The upshot was that while the lot remained valuable, the house had to be completely torn down. In the end, Joan got less for the property, adjusted for inflation, after 10 years than she originally paid for it.

TRAP

In this true example, Joan really did take advantage of elderly sellers, although probably not in a way that could get her into serious trouble. However, in general, especially when dealing with the elderly in real estate, it is important not to exert "undue influence." That simply means that you should not take advantage of anyone because of your relationship with him or her.

TIP

If you get a better deal because of a defect in the house, get the defect fixed. For example, although Ted and Sally got $10,000 off the price because of a problem roof in our earlier example, Ted did fix the problem, even though he did it for far less money. If Joan had taken care of the settling problem when she purchased the house, she probably would not have had a major problem years later.

The Bottom Line

The home inspection report can be a useful negotiating tool to leverage price in a real estate deal. However, it can be a double-edged sword. Sometimes it can help the buyer . . . and other times the seller.

11

How to Negotiate with a Lender

Most people believe that you can't negotiate with a lender. You take what they have to offer or not. It's that simple. For example, Nicole was buying her first home, a condo, and needed to secure financing. The price was $240,000 and she wanted to put no more than 5 percent down. That meant that she needed a 95 percent loan. She went to a mortgage broker who told her that while he could, indeed, secure a 95 percent mortgage for her, it would cost 1½ percent above the current market rate. This was because she had a blemish on her credit record and she couldn't get a prime loan. Thus, he'd have to go to a subprime lender.

TIP

Prime means the loan meets or conforms to mortgage underwriter standards for sale on the secondary market, usually Fannie Mae or Freddie Mac. These are the least expensive loans. Subprime loans are made by lenders who specialize in borrowers with credit problems, and they charge more for the mortgage.

In addition, the broker said he wanted three points (3 percent of the mortgage) as a loan fee plus another $1,000 in origination costs. And he wanted another $1,035 up front for handling the financing ($1,000 was an advance on the loan fees; the $35 was for a credit report).

Nicole, not knowing any better, agreed. The mortgage broker seemed to take forever to get the loan, but he finally did. But when it came time to sign, Nicole discovered that the loan was an extra 1 percent higher in interest and an extra point higher.

She protested, but the broker pointed out that the market had changed and this was the best he could do. Nicole said she wasn't satisfied and would go elsewhere. He smiled and replied that she was free to do that. But he had secured financing for her and was entitled to the $1,035 he had originally charged, whether she took the loan or not. Further, to go somewhere else meant having to start the whole financing process over again from the beginning. He wondered aloud if the seller would be willing to wait more weeks for her to secure a mortgage somewhere else.

In the end, she took the loan, paid the extra costs, and got the condo she wanted.

TIP

The Real Estate Settlement Procedures Act (RESPA) requires lenders to give borrowers a preliminary estimate of their costs for a mortgage. Read this statement carefully as it may reveal many of the "garbage fees" the lender may be charging.

When to Negotiate for a Mortgage

Nicole's problems (a true story by the way) stem from several misconceptions on her part. Like most people, she believed there was no possibility of negotiating with the lender. Then, when she was delivered an ugly mortgage that she didn't want, she attempted to negotiate anyway to get the mortgage broker to change the terms. By that time it was too late.

The truth is that everything in real estate is up for negotiation, including financing. However, you have to do the negotiations up front, not at the back end. At the beginning, when you first approach a mortgage broker (or direct lender such as a bank), you have the leverage. You can easily walk out and try somewhere else. You hold the high cards.

However, once the mortgage is ready to fund, you are at a disadvantage because you need the loan to close the deal and usually don't have time to begin searching elsewhere. Now the lender holds the high cards.

Lock Ins

Negotiate all the terms of the mortgage when you first approach the mortgage broker or lender. Then get a *lock in* that guarantees what you agreed upon. This assures you that you'll get the loan as agreed when it comes time to close your deal. Sometimes however, in a volatile market, lenders won't honor their own lock ins. To help reduce problems, get the lock in in writing.

Remember, in real life there is no such thing as an absolutely guaranteed lock in. For example, sometimes interest rates rise dramatically between the time you apply for the mortgage and the time to actually fund it. Perhaps they started at 5 percent and now they're at 6.5 percent. Your lender gave you a written 30-day lock in at 5 percent. That means that you have 30 days to close in order to get that rate.

You're ready to close in 30 days and demand the mortgage. The lender smiles and says okay. But there are delays. Your documents get lost in the mail. Suddenly a problem over your credit arises. Before you know it, it's 31 days. Astonishingly, the documents previously lost suddenly reappear and the credit blemish vanishes. "But," the lender sadly says, "it's past your lock-in time, so now the rate is higher."

The truth is no one, including a lender, wants to lose money. And if a little shuffling of paper or maybe a smudge on a credit report can keep that from happening, a few lenders will seize the opportunity. A reputable lender, of course, will honor a mortgage lock in no matter what. The trouble is, you usually don't know how reputable your lender is until it's too late.

What to Negotiate in a Mortgage

To put yourself in a position to negotiate with a lender, you have to remember that the lender is not doing you any kind of a favor by lending you money. It's a mutually (or should be) beneficial transaction. You need money; the lender needs interest. If your needs match, it's a deal. Strictly business. Thus, when you march into a mortgage broker or direct lender's office, you're on equal footing. You need each other.

TIP

It's usually more difficult to negotiate with a direct lender such as a bank or savings and loan because you generally don't get the opportunity to talk to the right person. You usually talk to a loan salesperson who simply mouths the lender's policy. "We have loan A, loan B, or loan C. Take your pick." If you can get in to see an officer who has discretionary powers, it is possible to get a loan tailored to your needs. That's why it's sometimes best to deal with a small lending institution instead of a giant one—or better still, a mortgage broker who has the ear of the lender.

Conforming or Nonconforming?

Perhaps the first thing to determine is whether or not you qualify for a conforming loan. As noted earlier, a conforming loan is one that meets the underwriting standards of Freddie Mac or Fannie Mae, the two huge quasi-government secondary lenders.

As of this writing, these mortgages cannot be for more than $359,650. Further, the underwriter sets the parameters of the loan—the minimum down payment, minimum credit score, and other qualifications. These mortgages are resold on the secondary market by the lender with whom you deal in large groups of loans. And generally the interest rate is set by the terms of that sale.

Thus, if you qualify for a conforming loan (because it usually is the best deal out there), there's very little leeway to negotiate with the lender. But there is some. For one thing, you can argue over the "garbage fees," largely unnecessary costs some lenders tack on to boost their profits. The lender must give you an estimate of these as soon as you apply for the loan. For another, you can negotiate the interest rate/points mix. (Remember, a point is equal to 1 percent of the mortgage amount and is paid up front.) When comparing points and interest rates, it's usually the case that points are equal to roughly one-fourth to one-eighth of a percent in interest. Thus, if you want to lower the interest rate, you can offer to pay more points. If you want fewer points, you can offer to pay a higher interest rate.

TIP

What the lender is actually looking for is *yield*. This is the true return on the mortgage from all sources, including points and rate. It is close to what you see when you are told the APR (annual percentage rate). The lender is looking to get a certain yield. As long as you can give that yield, you can often jostle the mix used to get it in a variety of ways.

TRAP

Check out the mortgage finance market just as you check out the real estate market. Local papers often report on the volume of financing in the real estate section of papers. Local real estate brokers can also tell about this market, as can mortgage brokers, who often are quite candid about conditions. If you hear that new financing and refinancing are at all time highs, figure you have little room to negotiate. On the other hand, if you read that lenders are laying people off because there is so little financing, your negotiating room just took a big jump.

Nonconforming Loans

Your ability to negotiate a nonconforming loan may be significantly better than it would be with a conforming loan. Nonconforming loans may be subprime loans (offered to those with credit problems) or portfolio loans (those kept by a financial institution in its loan "portfolio," hence the name). If the lender is going to hold the mortgage itself, then the parameters are determined by the lender . . . and may be widely negotiable. On the other hand, if yours is a subprime loan, then the lender will often, and sometimes arbitrarily, jack up both the points and interest rate it demands. You can, of course, argue. You can point out that you're a better credit risk than the lender is assuming based on information you could submit (such as that you were out of work for a time because of illness, but you're now well and holding down a steady job).

You may negotiate price, points, terms, and other costs with both portfolio and subprime lenders. Depending on the market (how many applications they have), they may be surprisingly flexible. These lenders are eager to make secure loans, often to the point of being highly competitive. If you're a good wheeler and dealer and can show why yours is a particularly secure loan, you may get a better rate and terms.

Do They Want to Lend You Money?

The bottom line is that when you go to a lender—be it bank, savings and loan, credit union, mortgage banker, or someone else—it's not that you're asking for a favor. The lender wants to give you a mortgage. After all, that's how they make their profit. If there are no borrowers, they are out of business. Thus, once again, things become negotiable. Often it's just a matter of getting to the person who will listen . . . and who has the power to make a decision.

12

Negotiating without an Agent

As I touched upon in Chapter 3, it is not necessarily true that the buyer, the seller, or both are not skilled negotiators and the real estate agent is.

Although most agents probably are skilled at negotiations (one would hope so since negotiating is part of their trade), not all agents are. Some make a handsome living simply by listing property and hoping that others will close the deal for them. A few simply muddle through the negotiations, letting their buyer or seller down by not negotiating strongly.

Just because you like an agent and he or she does well at showing you properties or at gaining your confidence in listing does not mean that he or she is able to do a good job for you at the negotiating table. You may be more skilled at negotiations—particularly after reading this book—than your agent. If that's the case, I suggest you could do a better job for yourself by dealing directly with the buyer/seller rather than letting the agent do the negotiating for you.

I'm not saying you shouldn't use an agent in a real estate deal. The agent's principal duty is to find a buyer for a seller. If an agent finds someone willing to buy your property (or finds a property you want if you're a buyer) and you help with the negotiations to close the deal, the agent, in my opinion, is still entitled to a commission.

However, if you feel that you're a skilled negotiator (chances are you won't feel that way unless you've had some successes in negotiating), then you might very well be the best person to present the purchase offer to the seller (or to come to the buyer with your counteroffer). I realize this flies in the face of conventional wisdom, but, then again, are you interested in justifying convention or getting the deal?

In real estate, probably negotiations for 90 percent of all deals are handled by agents. But not all. Some of the more spectacular deals made have been done by the buyer and seller working face-to-face, provided at least one of them is a skilled negotiator.

What If the Agent Throws Up a Roadblock?

If you're a buyer, your agent may say that you can't present the offer directly to the seller and that the seller has specified that he or she wants to deal only with a broker. (The seller's agent may make the same appeal with regard to presenting a counteroffer to the buyer.)

That's usually a lot of hooey. Most times the seller/buyer doesn't care who presents the offer. The agent's just trying to protect the deal (making the assumption that you'll blow it) or afraid of somehow losing a commission. (If the seller is tied up in the commonly used "right to sell" listing, it doesn't matter who presents the offer— the commission is still due the agent.)

If you demand to present the offer, I don't see how an agent can stop you. If the other party has indeed requested that only an agent present the deal, then you can agree to have the other party's agent present (sort of as protection). If the seller absolutely refuses to see you, you can make this offer, "I will buy your house. But you must deal with me directly." Put up a big earnest money deposit along with a signed contract and, except in a hot market, I can't imagine a seller not talking directly to you. In a hot market, sellers have so many buyers making offers they can stand back and pick and choose.

Never Believe Anyone Else Is Entirely on Your Side

Trust in yourself. You're the only person in the world who has your own interests totally at heart. This applies not only to the other party in the negotiations, but also to your agent.

When Would You Be Better Off Negotiating Directly?

A lot depends on whom the agent represents. Does he or she represent you or the other party? If the agent represents the seller, then he or she cannot fully represent the buyer and vice versa. Thus, in most states today we have strictly seller's agents and strictly buyer's agents. In some states there is a confusing combination where the agent has both the buyer and the seller sign a statement saying that he or she represents them both, except not entirely and not in every situation. This is called a "dual agency."

TRAP

I firmly believe that no one can serve two masters faithfully at the same time. No agent can faithfully serve both buyer and seller. If the agent represents the seller, than he or she cannot fully represent the buyer and vice versa. Yet many agents appear to do so.

Be sure you determine for whom your agent works. If you're a buyer and the agent is working for the seller, be careful of confiding your thoughts on price and terms to him or her. Your agent has a fiduciary responsibility to reveal your confidences to the seller! The same holds true if you're a seller talking to a buyer's agent. If the agent presumes to represent both parties, then probably neither party should confide.

All of which comes down to the fact that if the agent with whom you're dealing is not your fiduciary, then you might be wise to deal directly with the other party. Or get an agent who is loyal only to you.

TIP

Most buyers and sellers use agents as a kind of financial "Dutch uncle" to try out prices or terms they might consider. There's nothing wrong with this, so long as the agent is your fiduciary. Watch out, however, if the agent is working for the other party.

Can an Agent Work Against You?

Even if you're working with an agent who is presumably strictly on your side, there are still some subtle, sometimes unconscious conflicts of interest that can crop up. Remember that an agent works in a community, and it's to his or her advantage to see that every deal is a good deal for all concerned. The reason an agent wants things to work out this way is, simply put, repeat business. He or she wants to continue doing business in the community, wants recommendations (the bread and butter for new clients)—in short, wants to maintain a reputation.

This desire for a "fair deal" every time has some interesting ramifications in negotiations that are not always to your advantage. Let's say you're a buyer who, naturally, wants to get the lowest possible price on a house you want to purchase. (Obviously, this is the desire of every buyer.)

An agent shows you a suitable house and you decide you want to make an offer. Only, you want to lowball it. You want to offer far less than the asking price. So, you explain your offer to your agent and, further, state that you want to give the seller a 24-hour deadline to decide—no more. (See Chapter 2 on controlling time.)

The agent balks at this and argues against it. She says that the offer is ridiculously low; the seller won't even consider it; and it's not worth presenting. Further, the short deadline is a bad idea. She argues you can't "push people around like that. You have to be fair and give them time to consider." In short, she doesn't want to present your offer.

Now, is the agent looking out for your best interests? In some circumstances a lowball offer accompanied by a short deadline can be very effective. This is especially the case where the seller has had few or no other offers and is desperate to sell.

But, if the agent doesn't want to present the deal, I would suspect that the real reason is that she isn't comfortable in pressuring sellers. The lower the offer and the shorter the deadline certainly make her job harder.

There's also her reputation at stake. She probably doesn't want to be known in the business as someone who brings in lowball offers. It could affect the agent's ability to list other properties in the community. (Would you list with someone who brings you very low offers?)

So she attempts to discourage you. She says she wants the best deal for *both* you and the seller. But, do you really care if it's the best deal for the seller? Or are you concerned about getting the best deal for you?

How can you count entirely on this agent? She may, indeed, want to do the best for you. But conflicting with that may be her timidity and/or desire to maintain a reputation in a community among sellers and other agents.

Remember that for you, however, it's a one and only deal. You'll probably never see this seller again. Most likely you don't have a reputation as a real estate negotiator to worry about. (Indeed, the better the deal you make, the more respect you're likely to get from your peers.) Further, you can't count on making up on the next deal what you lose on this one. For you this is a "one shot," and it's to your advantage to get the best deal possible.

In short, your interests and those of your agent could be in conflict.

What is a good agent going to do in this situation? I've known agents whom I consider to be excellent who, when faced with taking in an offer that they really didn't want to present because of personal reasons, would do the right thing and simply tell such a buyer, "I'm sorry, but I really can't represent you. I think you'd be happier with some other agent." In other words, they realized they couldn't act in the best interests of the buyer and bowed out.

On the other hand, I've also known agents who would continue to work with buyers (or sellers) no matter what, even when they weren't representing them faithfully. The agent may indeed take in the offer, but only make a halfhearted presentation, which will surely not get the sale. You could lose the purchase not because of your offer, but because of your agent.

TIP

When your agent starts arguing that he or she doesn't want to present the offer you're ready to make, it's time to think about presenting the offer yourself—or getting a new agent.

TRAP

There's a very fine line between advice that's in your interest and coercion. A good agent may indeed point out that it could be to your advantage to make an offer or to counter and may even suggest what he or she considers to be a realistic price. On the other hand, a not so good agent may use a variety of arguments to bully or even scare you into making an offer that you really don't want to make.

If you ever find you are negotiating with an agent over the kind of offer or counteroffer to make, you are being pressured. The agent should present alternatives, not insist on what's best for you. If the agent insists, it could be that he or she is really insisting on what's best for the agent.

This is not to suggest that you should never trust your broker. It's only to point out that you should never put all of your trust in any other person in a business transaction.

13

Negotiating with a Builder

Most people believe that it's impossible to negotiate with home builders. (In this chapter, we're talking about builder/developers who put up spec homes for resale, not an individual builder you hire to construct a home for you.) This is understandable, since the builders sometimes go to great lengths to create that impression. However, as we've seen in this book, everything in real estate is negotiable.

With a builder, however, how much leverage you have often depends not so much on what you say as on the market conditions at the time. A decade ago builders across the country were starving, with thousands of homes sitting unsold. They were practically ready to give them away to anyone who would make an offer.

Today, as this is written, it's a different world. Prices in most areas are accelerating and there are many buyers for relatively few new homes. Many builders are sitting pretty, able to sell everything they put up.

Nevertheless, it's not all peaches and cream in the building industry. In some areas, things have slowed down just as building increased, and builders are again sitting on properties, happy to negotiate.

TIP

As with buying a car, a lot depends on the builder or car dealer you choose. You'll always get a better deal when there are homes sitting unsold or unpurchased cars on a lot.

Getting Negotiations Started

For most people, perhaps the hardest part of negotiating with a builder is getting the process started. Remember, the builder knows what you have in mind and, in most cases, has taken care to see that you are discouraged from negotiating.

Typically there are "set prices" for the various models, sort of like the way mayonnaise is priced on a grocery store shelf. And there are set prices for upgrades and options. In many cases, there are specific mortgage packages already in place that you are encouraged to use. For example, you may be told that if you want to pay all cash (get your own financing), the builder will be happy to sell to you. But, it will cost you more money in appraisal and lending fees, and it will be much easier simply to get the financing the builder already has in place.

TRAP

A builder may try to insist that you get a mortgage through its company as a condition of sale. You should resist such unethical tactics.

Further, the salesperson will often tell you that he or she is authorized to accept only full-price offers on the terms and conditions specifically written out. In other words, the implication is that nobody negotiates price, terms, and so on with builders.

When dealing with a builder, the method I use is to submit a prepared offer. You can either do it directly yourself or through an agent. If you use an agent, however, be aware that the builder may not be willing to pay an agent's fee and you may end up having to pay it yourself.

If you submit it yourself, I suggest you write up an offer (using expert counsel such as an attorney or competent agent) and bring it into the builder's sales office. The representative there should be a licensed real estate agent and should know the rules of the game. Accompany your offer by a reasonable deposit and tell the agent you would like to submit it to the builder/owner.

The agent may be very pleasant and quickly agree to do so, telling you he or she will let you know as soon as possible. I suggest you state that you want to present it in person. After all, you should have some negotiating tricks up your sleeve after reading this book. Again, they may readily agree.

On the other hand, the salesperson may stonewall you. I once had a salesperson say the builder absolutely would refuse to consider any offer that was not accompanied by a $10,000 cashier's check. The agent refused to let me speak to the builder and refused to accept my offer. I was able, however, to get the name of the builder (it was blazoned in huge letters on a sign outside) and I called direct. I spoke first to a secretary, explaining I had a cash offer (down payment plus financing on my end, cash to the builder) and then was connected directly to the builder, who invited me in. We eventually did not make a deal, but it wasn't because I couldn't speak to the builder/owner or because he insisted on a ridiculous sort of deposit.

TRAP

Beware of salespeople who are officious. Normally real estate agents will go out of their way to be helpful and courteous. But I have encountered a few salespeople at builders' offices who seem to have an attitude problem. It's as though they feel they're going out of their way to work with you. If you encounter those people, I suggest you try an end run as explained above.

What You Can Negotiate

With a builder you can negotiate price, terms, options, and extras. Keep in mind, however, that often an individual owner on a resale has more flexibility than a builder. An owner may have been in the house for years and built up a considerable equity. If you offer 15 percent less than asking price, the owner may be willing to consider it.

However, tract builders usually work on much thinner margins. They may have only 10 or 15 percent into the property after all costs are accounted for (including the costs of holding inventory). Thus, if you offer 15 percent below asking price, the builder may not be able to comply with your offer, even if he or she truly wants to. On the other hand, builders frequently have a huge mark up on options—and particularly upgrades. They can often be very flexible when negotiating these.

TIP

Sometimes you can find a home in a development that already has the upgrades/options put into it. Perhaps they were put in for an earlier buyer whose deal fell through. The builder will very likely be anxious to get rid of this home and may be very flexible when negotiating for those upgrades/options.

Understanding the Builder's Costs

When dealing with an individual on a resale, you as a buyer often want to know how long the house has been on the market, under the often correct assumption that the longer the time, the more desperate the seller is to get a sale.

With a builder, the situation is even more extreme. A builder must pay interest each month on unsold homes in inventory. Typically the spec builder will have included an allowance for this—say three to four months. If the homes get sold sooner, there's an additional profit. But, even if it takes four months, there's no loss.

Problems for builders arise when their inventory sits there unsold for long periods of time. Their holding costs can eventually drive them into bankruptcy. Therefore, the longer a fully constructed home has been sitting there unsold, the more your leverage increases. If it's been finished for six months, you should have lots of leverage.

TIP

You can determine how long the house had been completed by going into the garage and finding the building permit sign-off sheet. Usually these are tacked to a wall inside and remain there until a buyer is found for the property. They will contain dates and the signature of building inspectors. Look for the word *final* and the sign-off date.

When you find a builder who is under pressure from unsold homes, feel free to apply more pressure. Check back into the early chapters of this book and begin negotiations for price and terms. You may be surprised at how much you can get.

Negotiating for Options

Frequently, while builders may have little flexibility when it comes to price, they have enormous flexibility when it comes to a home's options. These include everything from carpeting upgrades to installing fences.

The basic rule when negotiating for options is: You can't get what you want until you first know what that is. In order words, as opposed to buying resales, where you spend a great deal of time trying to find something existing that will fill your needs and desires, with a builder you can often get it built to suit.

No, that doesn't mean that the builder is going to dramatically change his or her construction plans to accede to your every whim. But it does mean that if you get involved with a builder during the construction process, you can often choose the color of the interior of the home, the quality of the carpeting, kitchen counters and cabinets, and frequently a few design features such as whether a basement or attic is built out or left rough or whether a kitchen has recessed ceiling lights or a window planter is built in. In other words, unlike a resale where what you see is what you get, with new construction there is more flexibility.

NOTE: There's not as much flexibility as some people think with regard to changing options. Speculative builders (those who build first and hope to find a buyer later) typically will have a set of basic plans that have been approved by the local building department and by lenders for a certain mortgage amount. Further, the builder knows, sometimes to the dollar, how much everything will cost in terms of labor and material. To vary from these basic plans would mean delays and potentially very high extra costs for the builder. Hence, it's unlikely you'll get a builder to, for example, agree to change the basic layout of a home. A builder won't want to add a nook here or a bedroom there. You won't be converting a one story to a two story or the other way around. Yes, you can make minor changes, but very often not major ones. If a builder does agree, you can be sure it's going to cost you megabucks.

TIP

If you want to make changes that involve "design," you're probably better off buying a lot and then either hiring an architect and builder to create just what you want or doing the design and construction work yourself. But be prepared to pay more, lots more. Custom work always costs more than ready built.

Making a List of What You Want.   Before getting directly involved in negotiating with the builder, it's very useful to create a list of exactly what you want. Remember, you won't get it unless you know what it is. Here's a partial list of items over which you would typically have some choice in new home constructions.

Indoor Options

- Appliances (quality, color)
- Cabinets (material, quality, color)
- Carpet (quality, color)
- Carpet padding (quality)
- Countertops (material, quality, color)
- Doors (hollow or solid core, material, quality)
- Finishings (railings, handles, light switches, etc.)

- Flooring in entry, kitchen, bath (material, color)
- Light fixtures (design, quality)
- Mirrors (location, size, quality)
- Paint (color, quality)
- Plumbing fixtures—toilet, sink, etc. (quality, color)
- Rough or finished extra rooms
- Windows (quality, planter box)

Outdoor Options

- Driveway (material, width)
- Fencing (complete, partial, or none)
- Insulation (more)
- Lot (location and/or size)
- Roof (material, quality, color)
- Walls (material, quality, color)
- Yard (landscaped front/back, quality)

As you can see, there are many choices. It's a good idea to visit several developers' models to get an idea of what's being offered in your area. As you go, note those items that appeal to you, then add them to your list. When you finally come to the builder whose home you want to purchase, you should have a fairly complete idea of those items that you must have, those that you would like to have, and those that you can live without.

The "Upgrade" Trap. Builders, of course, understand exactly what you, as a buyer, are doing. They know that you are looking around at this model and that and are aware that you are making a list of your options. They know you are doing it, and they are prepared for you. It would be hard to find a builder of spec houses who didn't have his or her own list of "upgrades" and "options."

The *options* are design changes that builders have anticipated buyers might want and for which they have already received building department and lender approval. They also know their exact cost. You want a love seat in the family room, no problem. They can put it in. You want a skylight in the master bedroom, no problem. You can have it. All for more money, of course.

Similarly, there are *upgrades*, a list of items the builder can change in terms of material, quality, and color. You want thicker carpet, again no problem. You want granite countertops instead of tile, it can be handled . . . all for more money.

What should be obvious is that there are actually two issues here. The first is the breadth and depth of the builder's list of options and extras. The second is cost. We'll deal with each separately.

The Builder's List. As I noted earlier, the builder must get approval for most changes from the building department and the lender. Further, a good builder will have penciled in all the costs for labor and material for the basic plan, as well as any options and upgrades. The number of items and the variety offered will differ from builder to builder. A good builder, however, will have a lot of options and upgrades available. Typically, the higher priced the home, the larger the list.

Arguing over the Builder's List. Although builders are normally quite willing to grant you any item on *their* lists—at a price—as noted earlier, they are extremely unhappy about adding something not on their lists. This can result in some strange arguments. For example, this actually happened to a friend of mine. The builder had a series of colors from Sherwin-Williams. But the color my friend wanted was from Sears. For some reason, the builder just didn't have the right shade on his list. My friend suggested that as a solution, the builder get the paint from Sears, but the builder insisted it had to be from Sherwin-Williams. (Note: the roles of the two paint companies could just as easily be reversed. The point here is not that either has better paint or more colors. They both offer excellent products.) As it turned out, the builder was probably locked into a price and had already agreed to purchase a certain amount of paint. He or she never acceded to my friend's wishes.

This can occur with any option or upgrade. You want a particular brand of carpeting. But the builder offers a different brand. For the same reasons, getting the builder to switch brands is going to be very tough.

In short, if what you have on your wish list coincides with what's on the builder's available options/upgrades list, your chances of negotiating for it are excellent. On the other hand, wherever the two lists differ, you're in for a fight.

Negotiating Costs

The other part of this equation is the cost to you. This will often become most clear with regard to carpeting. Today, many new homes offer wall-to-wall carpeting. However, often the padding is very light and the carpeting is of a low quality. Many home buyers want to upgrade both.

If you want to upgrade, the builder may smile and direct you to the "design center." This is usually a showroom at either the model homes or sometimes at a commercial store located off site. Here you will be shown a variety of colors, patterns, and qualities. The trouble is the price.

In my experience, the price at the design center is often two or three times higher than what you could get the same carpeting for elsewhere on your own. It may quickly become pretty evident that the builder has added a significant profit to the upgrades.

TRAP

Just as when cars are sold, there may be more profit in the add-ons than in the basic product.

At this point, many would-be buyers will say something like, "We don't like your choice of carpeting. We'd prefer to get our own."

"Fine," the builder may reply. "However, you'll have to get your own *after* you move in." In other words, you'll have to take up and discard the builder's carpeting to put in your own, a costly and wasteful procedure.

"No," you may protest. "We want to put our own carpet in place of yours . . . and since you won't be putting in any carpet, we'd like a credit."

At this point, the builder may snicker and say something like, "Not on your life!" The explanation may go something like this: In order to sell the property, the lender requires that it be completed, and that includes all carpeting down and in place. The builder cannot sell the home and you cannot get a new mortgage without carpeting down. This is usually very true.

As a consequence, if you want to put your own carpeting in, it would have to be done *before* you buy. This has some serious complications. What happens, for example, if at the last minute you can't complete the transaction? Do you lose the money you paid for the carpeting? Does the builder need to pay you back? (Unlikely.) Further, if you buy it yourself and pay for it to be laid yourself, there is the question of mechanics' liens that the builder has to worry about. (If it turns out you have a disagreement with the carpet people and don't pay, will the builder be liable for the costs even after you buy?)

As you can see, there are many roadblocks that the builder can raise in front of you. It will seem so much easier simply to go to the design center and pay the outrageously high price for upgrades or options.

It doesn't have to be that way. You could have the builder buy the carpeting you want and install it. There would be no problem with mechanics' liens that way. Further, you could give the builder a non-refundable check to cover a large portion of the amount between your discount on the builder's carpeting and the cost of your choice. Of course, you would be at risk of losing your money if the deal didn't go through. But if you only paid a portion, the builder would be at some risk too and would certainly want you to get the home. And you could get the carpeting laid at the last minute to reduce the risk of the deal's not going through.

Getting an Option Discount.   The simplest method, of course, is to go with the carpeting that the builder has already selected (chances are you'll find something there that you like) and insist that it be given to you at a discount. Don't hesitate to ask for a huge discount, like 50 or 75 percent. Remember, the builder is getting it at cost and often has added enormous markup.

TIP

It may be easier to get a huge discount on upgrades and options than a price reduction on the house.

It all comes down to how well you negotiate with the builder (see the earlier chapters) and how motivated he or she is to move the property. With a well-motivated builder—usually one who has a large unsold inventory—amazing things are possible.

Mortgage Buy Downs

In the days of higher interest rates (as happens periodically), the reason that builders can't sell their homes is that people can't qualify for mortgages. As an inducement to purchase, therefore, sometimes builders will be willing to negotiate a *buy down.*

In a buy down, the builder gives a certain amount of cash to a lender at the time you get a mortgage and, in return, the lender offers you a lower interest rate. Typically the lower rate varies. For example, it could be 3 percent lower than market the first year, 2 percent the second, 1 percent the third, and at market the fourth.

This reduction will lower your monthly payments, often significantly, and make it far easier for you to qualify. Indeed, you may be thinking that you're getting a real bargain here.

What's important to keep in mind, however, is that there's no free meal in real estate. What is given away by one hand is often taken back by the other. The builder may have increased the price of the home to offset the buy down on the mortgage. This means you could end up paying more for the property in order to get a lower interest rate.

Of course, as a good negotiator, you'll go for both a lower rate and a better price.

The Bottom Line

Yes, you can negotiate price, terms, options, and upgrades with a builder. But your success will often be determined not only by how well you handle the negotiations, but also by the market conditions at the time and, specifically, how successful at selling new homes the builder happens to be.

14

How to Bargain for Personal Property

Often buyer and seller will negotiate over more than just the house itself. At stake may be a dining room chandelier, a refrigerator or stove, a washer and dryer. Even children's outdoors swings may be up for grabs. I recently sold a home in which I had put an L-shaped bench into a small kitchen alcove. It fit perfectly and really did make the room attractive. However, it was a piece of furniture and did not go with the house. I properly informed the buyers of that fact.

The buyers, however, could not see themselves living in the home without my table and bench. So they wrote it into the offer. They wanted to buy my house *and* those items of furniture. They made it a deal point.

Quite frankly, I wasn't all that concerned about the furniture. It hadn't cost that much, and I really didn't know where else I could put it. However, as long as the buyers wanted it, and apparently wanted it badly, I was willing to negotiate. I happened to need extra time to move. So I offered to trade off. They could have the table and bench, but I got to stay an extra 20 days after the deal closed without paying rent. They said fine, which was just great for me since rent for that piece of property for that time would have been several times the cost of a new table and bench!

TRAP

It's usually not a good idea from the buyer's perspective to have a seller remain in the property after the close of escrow. However, there's nothing illegal or unethical about it, and if it's a deal point, the buyer may accept it.

What Is Personal Property?

It's important to understand the technical distinction between *real* and *personal* property. *Real property* refers to the land and anything attached to the land, including the house, fences, separate garage, sheds, and so forth.

Personal property generally refers to anything that you can take with you, such as clothing, furniture, children's toys, computers, TVs, clothes washers and dryers, refrigerators, and so forth.

There is also a gray area that is very important in real estate because it sometimes causes confusion, which can lead to bitter squabbles between buyer and seller. Consider the following true example.

Peter and Rita made an offer that was accepted on a home that was about seven years old. What Peter and Rita really liked about the house, in addition to its location and layout, were the expensive wooden blinds on all the windows. This gave the house a rich, modern look that very much appealed to them. They also liked the built-in refrigerator and stove/oven in the kitchen.

The escrow did not seem unusual, and the sale concluded within about five weeks. The buyers had not asked for a walk-through. (They were out of town at the time and, besides, the sellers were extremely neat and tidy people, so Rita and Peter figured the house would be left in good shape.)

A few days after the close of escrow, when Peter and Rita walked into their new home, they were aghast. It was clean and neat as a pin. However, all the wooden blinds were gone—the sellers had taken them. In addition, the sellers had taken the built-in refrigerator and stove/oven.

It took the buyers milliseconds to get on the phone and contact the agent, who was likewise surprised. She contacted the sellers, who explained as follows: They had left the screws and attachment assemblies for the blinds. But the blinds themselves had not been in any way permanently attached to the house. So the sellers considered them personal property and took them. They were using them in their own new home.

Further, the so-called built-in kitchen appliances were simply sitting in wells in the counter. They, too, were not attached in any way—simply held in place by weight. They were easily removed and simply unplugged from electric sockets located under the counter. The sellers likewise considered these items personal property, took them, and planned to use them later on in another house they hoped to build.

Rita and Peter were horrified and angry. They said that one of the major reasons they had bought the property was the blinds and the built-ins. They wanted them returned immediately.

When the agent conveyed the message, the sellers simply replied, "If you wanted our personal property included in the deal, you should have specified it in the sales agreement. Barring that, those items are our personal property and we're keeping them."

The buyers were outraged, the sellers self-righteous. It appeared that the whole thing was headed for court. However, the agent, an old friend of mine, prevailed upon the sellers to be reasonable and the built-ins were returned. Then the agent paid for part of the cost of new blinds from his own pocket—an expensive lesson learned.

This true story occurred over 20 years ago and it's unlikely it would occur today. Modern sales agreements typically provide (or agents should write in) that included in the purchase are all wall, window, and floor coverings and built-ins. Further, there's the walk-through, which originated in part just because of this situation. Thus, today it's unlikely that Peter and Rita would find themselves in this sort of predicament.

However, the story does illustrate some of the gray areas between personal and real property. Very often, it's simply hard to tell. For example, is a swing set in the backyard real or personal property? What about an area rug in the living room? Or a vise on a workbench in the garage?

In real estate, the determination of gray areas often hinges on a variety of tests, including method of attachment and intent. For example, if the swing set is secured by being sunk into holes in the ground, then the attachment suggests permanence and it probably is real property. On the other hand, if the swing set is simply sitting on top of the ground, it suggests portability and it's probably personal property.

Similarly, an area rug simply lying on the floor is undoubtedly personal property. But if it's tacked down and removing the tacks will leave marks in the floor, it's probably real property.

TRAP

Sometimes you can inadvertently convert personal property to real. For example, you own your home and you buy an expensive vise and workbench that you nail into the wall of your garage. When you bought the vise and workbench, it was obviously personal property. However, by your method of attachment, you may have converted it to real property.

How Do You Negotiate to Get Personal Property Included in the Deal?

As a buyer, you may fall in love with a piece of personal property just as Rita and Peter did in our example. It could be a beautiful, bell-shaped glass chandelier in the dining room. Maybe it's a portable barbecue outside or a great child's gym set with a sandbox. It could be anything, including the seller's large-screen TV set, which fits just perfectly in the family room, or the hope chest that looks so good by the window in the master bedroom. It can even be the seller's silverware or water skis!

TIP

If you're interested in items of a truly personal nature such as silverware, water skis, or even clothing, most of the time it's best simply to buy these separately outside of the real estate sale. The reason is that when lenders see such items included in a sales agreement, they may devalue the real property by an amount they feel the items are worth. In other words, mortgage lenders aren't in the business of financing personal property.

TIP

On the other hand, items that could be considered necessary to the operation of the home, such as a built-in refrigerator, washer/dryer, and so on, usually will receive more liberal lender treatment.

If you as a buyer want certain personal property included in the deal, there are basically two approaches that you can take: subtle and direct. The subtle approach is not to let on to the seller how badly you want the item. Instead of "oohing" and "aahing" over kitchen window curtains, you can simply not mention them at all. Then, when you fill out the sales agreement, be sure that it states that all window coverings are included in the sale. Presumably that would take in the kitchen curtains, and when the seller agrees to the deal as written, they're yours. (You can check for them on the final walk-through.) Thus, you've negotiated very subtly and not made the curtains a deal point for which the seller might want a concession.

On the other hand, sometimes sellers will point out that certain items such as a wood-burning stove insert, which are in a gray area, are personal property, are going to be taken by the seller, and are nonnegotiable. Now you're going to have to deal directly with the issue.

TIP

The word *nonnegotiable* usually means that you can get it, but it will cost you something.

If you want a piece of personal property that the seller obviously intends to take away, you automatically make it a deal point. For example, you may include a statement in your sales agreement that says the wood-burning stove insert (*insert*, by the way, means that the stove fits inside an existing fireplace) is to be included as part of the sale.

By drawing attention to the insert, you've made it a deal point. If the sellers have already said that the insert is not included in the deal, or even if they haven't, they may refuse to let it go. They may accept your offer, but cross out and initial the paragraph that has to do with the insert. Now you're in full-blown negotiations.

If you've made the insert a deal point, it becomes a matter of, "What will it take to get you to give up that damn stove?" Maybe the sellers want to be paid more and maybe, if you really want it, you're willing. Or maybe the sellers want more time (as was my situation earlier). Or maybe the sellers want a better interest rate on a second mortgage they are carrying back and this is just another way of trying to get it.

Your choices here are to trade off or stand firm by trying to increase the pie. We've already discussed trading off. Increasing the pie means that you would attempt to demonstrate to the sellers why it's necessary to include the insert as part of the deal. Maybe the house is in a cold climate and all homes in the area come with some sort of wood-burning stove. It's accepted as a necessary item. You might point out that not to include the insert would actually lower the value of the property. You wouldn't buy a home that didn't have one, and chances are that neither will anyone else. That sort of logic may prevail with a reasonable seller.

How Do You Keep Personal Property Out of the Deal?

There's another perspective here, and that's the view of the seller. Thus far we've been seeing how a buyer can get a seller to throw in a piece of personal property. But how does a seller keep a buyer from demanding this?

The answer is really quite simple. Remove it before the property is put up for sale.

For example, not too long ago I sold a property in which I had installed a lovely and expensive porcelain and brass light fixture in the dining room. My wife and I had purchased the fixture on a vacation and it was a memento of our trip. We really wanted to keep it. Of course, we didn't want it enough to lose a sale.

The real problem, however, was how to keep the light fixture from becoming a deal point, since I suspected any buyer coming through would likewise want it and would insist upon it, even if we said it was our personal property and was "nonnegotiable."

The answer was simple. I went to a hardware store and bought another attractive, but inexpensive, light fixture and replaced the one we wanted to keep. Then I packed up the memento and put it out of sight.

Thus, when a buyer came to the house, there was only the new light fixture there. There could be no issue raised over the old fixture—it simply was no longer there.

Similarly, a friend of mine had a rather nice swing set installed in concrete in holes in his backyard. When it came time to sell, he wanted to take it with him to his next house. However, he had no place to store it in the meantime.

So, he dug out the swing set, filled the holes, and then laid it down on the ground in the backyard. He didn't go out of his way to mention it to buyers. But, because it was laying on top of the ground, not buried in it, it was obviously personal property and not real. After the house sold, he took it with him. The buyer actually did comment on the "missing swing set," but when it was pointed out that it was obviously personal property, the buyer did not pursue the matter.

TIP

Sometimes the best way to negotiate an issue is to remove it from the bargaining table before negotiations begin.

The Bottom Line

Anything, including personal property, is negotiable. As a buyer, you can often get an item of personal property included in a deal simply by asking for it or by trading for it. As a seller, you may be able to keep a personal item by simply removing it from sight.

Negotiating for personal property is very often a part of buying and selling a home. Just be sure that when you negotiate for it, you know what's at stake as well as what you have to win . . . and lose.

15

Prevail in an Appraisal Argument

There are two occasions when you're likely to get into an argument with an appraiser. The first and most common is when you're seeking a new mortgage, either to refinance or purchase, and the appraiser says the property isn't worth what you want for it. The second is when you get your property tax bill and you want to challenge it. We'll cover each separately.

What Do You Negotiate When a Lender's Appraiser Says "No!"?

I had a neighbor who, after her husband's death, decided she wanted to sell a vacation home that she and her husband had owned. She talked to a few brokers, got a feel for the market, and put it up for sale for $550,000. (It was, indeed, a very nice place on a river in the Sierra foothills of California.)

To be fully prepared, she called up an appraiser recommended by one of the brokers and paid for a formal appraisal so that she could tell any prospective buyer how she justified her price.

I lived nearby and happened to be there when the appraiser showed up. It was a nice warm morning and we walked around the property talking about real estate. After he had duly measured the lot and the house and written up the details of the home, we talked price. He said that in his opinion the property was not worth more than $230,000, tops. He had run a search for "comps" in the immediate area going back to the previous year and there hadn't been any recent sales. Therefore, he had gone to another development some 10 miles away and used it for comparables.

I pointed out to him that he was dealing with recreational property. That meant that demand for it was sporadic. A year or two might go by with no sales, then there might be one or two dozen sales in a matter of months. Further, I pointed out that the development he had used for comparables was not near the river and the community was not nearly as desirable.

He pointed out that the houses were of a similar age, design, and size. That was good enough for him. Since, after all, it wasn't any of my business, I demurred from saying more.

My neighbor, however, came to see me shortly afterward and told me how terrible the appraisal was. She had anticipated that the property would come in at the full price she was asking. Now, she was afraid she'd have to ask much less.

I suggested that she continue to ask her full price and when she got a buyer, let that buyer go to a lender and see what the appraisal was.

She did just that, and after a little over a month she accepted a full-price offer. For a mortgage, I suggested she tell the buyer to contact a local small bank with only three branches that did business in the county. I told her that since they were located nearby, they might be more aware of the true property values. She agreed and informed the buyer, who followed through.

The new lender sent out its own appraiser. Again, I was home when she came by and again I walked the property with her. I mentioned the previous appraiser and noted that he had used comps from a development some 10 miles away. I also pointed out that I thought they were invalid and suggested that she should instead use comps, no matter how old, from the present area. She agreed and found several sales 18 months earlier, all above $500,000. She sent in her report and my neighbor got a good loan commitment for 80 percent of the full sales price.

How Do You Challenge a Lender's Appraisal?

There are essentially two methods of challenging a bad (in your opinion) lender's appraisal. The above example lists one: go to a different lender, one who has some reason to see it your way.

TRAP

Arguing with a lender over the amount of an appraisal is a futile effort. Lenders are basically paper pushers. They need a piece of paper to prove the borrower's income, another to verify credit, and yet another to state the value of the property. They don't really care much about the real world. Just give them the papers that contain the right information and the borrower has a loan. But if the papers don't say the right things, the lender simply can't (or won't) act.

It's a somewhat different story when a lender comes in with a bad appraisal. Short of changing lenders, which may or may not be a possibility, you need to get the appraisal changed. As noted, arguing with the lender over the appraisal is futile. You need to get to the level of the appraiser. You need to get the lender to request a *reappraisal.*

Unfortunately, this is not always possible. Some lenders adamantly refuse to reappraise. In that case, you will either have to be satisfied with a lower loan or go elsewhere.

However, other lenders will request a reappraisal. To get them to do this, be prepared to go to the lending officer and argue that the original appraiser made a significant mistake (such as appraising the wrong property, not considering recent sales in the area, or not even coming into the home or looking at the yard). A little begging might work too.

If you get a reappraisal, it might cost you another fee. Of course, if you get a better appraised value, it could be worth it. Unfortunately, many lenders request that a reappraisal be done by the original appraiser, which means that you start off behind the eight ball. (You can request a new appraiser and some lenders will go along with you.) It's only human nature that the original appraiser, in order to preserve his or her reputation, is going to come out determined to prove the original figures were right. (On the other hand, you might get lucky and have a different appraiser who has no axe to grind.)

Either way, you need to get the property prepared. Yes, it's a good idea to get the house clean, mow the lawn, cut the shrubs, and plant some new flowers near the pathway. But, all of these items really don't amount to a hill of beans when it comes to appraisal. What counts is the size of the lot and house, the style, the general condition, and, most of all, *comparables*! (Remember, knowledge is king.)

That means that you need to do some investigating before the appraiser arrives. Work with one or more agents to find all sales of comparable homes in your area. Sales within the past six months are the most relevant, but if these are unavailable, go back further. Pending sales of homes (if you can find out the price) are also helpful. Get documentation of sales from a real estate agent (a printed list with an agent's office logo on top is usually enough). Also, take the time to go to each of the places and take a picture. It really is true that a picture is worth a thousand words. If the appraiser sees that the comparable looks just like your home, he or she is going to be hard pressed to deny it as a comparable. Thus, when the appraiser arrives, you will be well armed.

TIP

Be sure you're there to meet the appraiser. If you let him or her do it alone again, you might get the same negative result.

I suggest you remember the first rule of negotiating—make sure it's business, not personal. Be nice to the appraiser; don't be offensive by telling him or her what a miserable job he or she did on the first appraisal (even though it may be true).

If the appraiser wants to remeasure the house (as most will), go along and chitchat. But be sure you present your list of comparables, with their square footage, number of rooms, floor plan, location, style, and, most importantly, sales price. Hand it to the appraiser personally and, if possible, go over each one.

Most appraisers are honest, and if you've done your homework and were able to find comparables to justify your price, they will admit,

". . . maybe I overlooked these." If they accept your comparables, you may be in good shape. If they don't, you can complain to the lender again, although, as noted earlier, it won't do you much good.

TIP

Your documented complaint to the lender about an appraiser who won't change the price even when confronted with comparables won't do the appraiser any good either. Appraisers count on referrals from lenders and lenders want to make loans. If the lender suspects an appraiser of making and then hiding a mistake, that appraiser could spend a lot of time searching for new business. Appraisers know this and it's a great motivating force to correct an improper valuation.

TRAP

Because of the rise in value of most properties during the last few years, many lenders have told appraisers to be more conservative. They don't want to make loans that are too high. If the appraiser has a choice between two figures, it may be the lender who insists the lower figure be taken. There's no fighting this kind of logic.

A final word must be said regarding the cost of appraisal. Today, it's running in the $300 to $400 range. A reappraisal, as noted above, might cost you a second fee with no guarantee of a better result. However, it might be possible to split the costs. While the borrower/buyer normally pays for the initial appraisal, it wouldn't be unreasonable to ask the seller to pay for a reappraisal. After all, it's the seller's property value that is now holding up the transaction.

How Do You Challenge the State's Appraisal?

This is a rather different matter. Whenever you own real property, the state (or county) appraises it for tax purposes. These appraisals are typically made when the property is first improved (a home built on it), when it's sold, and, in some jurisdictions, every so many years thereafter. (In California, under Proposition 13, the state can only reevaluate the property upon new construction and sale.)

Rather than using an independent appraiser, often a county employee from the assessor's office is sent out to determine the value of your home for tax purposes. The method of appraisal is identical to that for a lender's appraisal. The size, condition, and, most of all, comparables are considered.

TIP

Be there, prepared, when the appraiser from the assessor's office shows up. These people have a lot of property to appraise and they don't like challenges to their appraisals, which slow down their work. Provide the appraiser with good solid reasons why your property is worth only as much as you think (using comparables to back yourself up). Sometimes, to avoid a challenge later on, the appraiser may be more than willing to consider your arguments.

Once the appraisal has been made, it is filed with the county assessor's office, and in due time (often several months), you will receive a notice telling you what the county feels your property is worth. The note may also give you a time and place for appealing the amount, although that's not always the case. (You can, however, always appeal, provided you meet the usually very strict time deadlines.)

TRAP

Some people receive their assessed valuation and are thrilled because it is so low—sometimes only half or a quarter of what they think the property is worth. Don't be fooled; you're dealing with politicians. There's also the "tax rate." This is the amount of tax you pay on your valuation. Politicians can agree to value property at half or a quarter of its true market value, then raise the tax rate so that you're paying as much as if the property had been valued at full market price. Most people only look at the valuation and don't pay attention to the rate.

Find out at what percentage of market value your house has been valued. (Call the assessor's office.) If it's half, then double the valuation figure to get how much the appraiser figured your house was worth. You could be unpleasantly surprised! Remember, here we're concerned about paying taxes—the lower the appraisal, the less the tax bite.

You will be given a time and place to appeal an assessed valuation of your property. Before you appear, go to the county assessor's office and ask to see their file on your property. (Don't be surprised to find it's only a three by five card. If it's a computer file, get a printout.) Check it carefully.

Be at the appeals hearing on time and be prepared. Don't argue emotionally; negotiate with facts. Some of the solid reasons that you can use to get an appeals board to change the valuation on your property are the following.

Examples of Reasons for Changing a Valuation

- *Wrong Comparables.*   Bring your own set of comparables with photos and a description of the comparables, including price, signed by someone such as a real estate agent.
- *Wrong Description.*   Assessors make mistakes. Maybe they said your house had four bedrooms when it only has three.
- *Wrong Calculations.*   Did the assessor get the right number of square feet for the house? What about for the lot? Remember, assessors are only human and most are severely overworked. Mistakes of this kind, unfortunately, are more common than people suspect.
- *Wrong Exemptions.*   You may be entitled to a variety of exemptions such as one for homeowners, for religious property, or for something else.
- *Wrong Extenuating Factors.*   Sometimes there will be a detracting feature that will reduce value that the assessor missed. For example, if your property is next to a toxic waste dump, it's likely to be worth significantly less than a comparable located

a mile away. Similarly, your property may have a utility easement running through the front lawn that could lower its value, and the assessor simply overlooked this.

How Do You Appeal an Improvement?

When you improve your property by, for example, adding a new room or putting on a new roof, you will likely get a new appraisal. Generally speaking, most counties will reevaluate your property at that time and often will significantly increase its value.

Again, appeal—first to the appraiser in person and then, if necessary, to the appeals board. It's very helpful to bring along all the receipts for what the improvement cost. Any appraiser is going to be hard put to argue that your new room addition added $40,000 to the value of your property when you can prove it only cost $5,000. (But many appraisers will make the argument that the new room added more to the value than simply its cost. At this point, the argument usually turns to comparables.)

TRAP

Be careful about improving more than 50 percent of your property. In many jurisdictions, when you improve more than half the value, the entire property can be reevaluated. If you have an existing low evaluation, it can now shoot up to current market values. If you keep the improvement to less than 50 percent, frequently only the part improved can be reassessed.

16

Negotiate on Investment Property

When negotiating real estate, most of the rules apply regardless of the type or size of the property, whether it's a single-family home, a strip mall, or a large office complex. However, when you get into investment property of one type or another, there are some additional deal points that you will want to consider.

A *deal point* is simply something negotiable on which the deal hinges. In a home sale, it might be the price or the time for occupancy. But in investment property it could be a variety of things from internal rate of return (cash on cash) to security deposits. While some are complicated concepts and are beyond the scope of this book, the art of negotiating them remains virtually the same. And that's what we'll deal with in this chapter.

Negotiating the Price of Income Property

There are many different methods of determining the value of an investment property. These include capitalizing the income of the property or determining the return on the actual cash invested. However, the most commonly used "quick method" for real estate income property is the *gross income multiplier*.

For example, Sam owns a 23-unit apartment building. His total rental income is $20,000 a month, or $240,000 annually. What's the value of Sam's building?

Sam may tell you that the gross income multiplier for his area is 10. Therefore, his property is worth $2,400,000. How did he arrive at this figure? He simply multiplied the gross annual income by 10 ($240,000 × 10 = $2,400,000). That's the value, according to Sam.

TRAP

Beware—the multiplier does not take into account the cost of borrowing money. Depending on interest rates and the amount financed, you may or may not be able to afford an income property, regardless of what the multiplier says it's worth.

TIP

When actually calculating the gross income multiplier, a percentage of the gross annual income is usually deducted for vacancies—sometimes 5 percent.

What should be apparent is that if the value of any property is going to be determined in large part by the multiplier, the question becomes, "How did Sam arrive at a figure of 10?" The amount of the gross annual multiplier, therefore, becomes a deal point to be negotiated. (After all, it will help determine the price.)

Knowledge, again, is king when negotiating. If you know how the multiplier was determined, you are a long way ahead of the other party, who doesn't. The multiplier is strictly a rule-of-thumb method, there is no set multiplier fixed in stone. It's what anybody thinks it is. Having said that, let me further say that the idea of a multiplier is a bit more scientific than I've made out and, properly used, can be quite helpful.

The multiplier is found by once again looking at comparables. Take the most recent sales of half a dozen comparable income properties. Then divide the actual sales price by the gross annual income and you have a multiplier. Take the average of all six properties' multipliers and you have a fairly accurate number that you can apply to your property.

If done as indicated above, the multiplier can be a very useful tool. In fact, I've found that it is extraordinarily accurate, as confirmed by other methods. Of course, negotiations revolve around how comparable the other properties are and what the current property's true gross annual income is (not always as easy to determine as it seems it should be).

TIP

Many owners and buyers, unfortunately, don't do a thorough job of researching comparables to come up with a true multiplier. Rather, they call up a few real estate agents and ask, "What's the income multiplier in this area?" The agent, who may or may not know anything about this, might say, "7," or "17," or whatever. Suddenly the number takes on mythic proportions and the buyer won't pay more or the seller accept less. Don't accept anyone else's word for the multiplier until you see it documented with comparables.

TRAP

Beware of "historic" multipliers. Sometimes an area will explode in value and multipliers will jump up. However, a year or so later, the explosion is over, and those multipliers may settle back down. Expect that sellers may still refer to the old numbers. Be sure you see that, whatever multiplier you use, it's current with the times.

How Do You "Negotiate" the Rents?

What should be obvious is that the value depends on at least two things: recent sales prices and the current rent from the property in question. While accurate recent sales prices of comparables should be fairly easy to obtain (call a few agents who deal in income property), determining the true gross income from rents for a specific property can be a bit trickier.

Pam was interested in buying a low-income seven-unit apartment building. The owner was using a multiplier of 14, which was conservative for the area. The owner said all units were filled, each was rented out for $650, and the gross annual income, therefore, was $54,600. That meant the building was worth (times 14) $764,400.

Pam felt that was a reasonable price and bought. However, the first month she discovered that three of the tenants were months behind in their rent and a fourth, a brother-in-law of the owner, was living there free. By the time she kicked all of the deadbeats out and rerented, Pam found her average monthly rental only brought in $500. For seven rentals that was only $42,000 annually. When the multiplier of 14 was used, the true value of the property was only $588,000, nearly $176,400 less than she paid!

Pam's story, unfortunately, is true more often than most people realize. Owners know that the way to inflate value is to get rents up any way they can. Too often, however, buyers find out the hard way that this has been done.

The true gross annual rent, therefore, like the gross income multiplier, is another deal point. Some investors I know use their own rule-of-thumb when negotiating here. When a seller tells them the gross annual rent is one figure, they simply discount that figure by 10 or sometimes 15 percent, then negotiate from there. They call this the "puff factor." The owner is puffing up the rents to make the property appear more valuable than it really is.

A better way of dealing with the problem, however, is to get a true reading of the rents. This can be accomplished in several ways. A buyer can examine the cash receipts of the seller for the year, or look at the rental agreements with the tenants, or, if necessary, contact each tenant individually before concluding the sale to determine how much rent is paid and how current payments actually are.

How Do You Negotiate over Deposits?

Deposits, the cleaning and security kind that tenants give to landlords to hold during the tenancy, may seem like small potatoes. But in recent years they have become increasingly important. In fact, in some cases they are the deal point around which a sale hinges. How can this be? It's all a matter of cash.

There's a very old joke that goes something like this. Sal and Pete are talking and Sal says, "I've got good news and I've got bad. Which do you want to hear first?"

Pete says, "What's the good news?"

To which Sal replies, "They've accepted our $10 million offer for the office building."

"Great," Pete replies, and then asks, "So, what's the bad news?"

Sal answers, "They want $500 in cash!"

The truth of the matter is that most investment property deals are heavily financed. The buyer frequently puts little cash money into the deal. But there is always a great need for cash—to pay off the agent's commission, the closing costs, and the seller.

In an income property transaction, except for new financing, the only real cash in the deal sometimes may come from security/cleaning deposits. Consider the following. There's a 25-unit apartment building. Rents are $1,000 a month, making the price roughly $6,000,000 (assuming a multiplier of 20). That's a fairly large number. But, chances are it's not a cash number. Presumably, the buyer is going to finance most of it, perhaps all of it, with even the seller carrying back a substantial amount of paper.

Except for the deposits.

Let's say that each apartment puts up one and a half times one month's rent in a cleaning/security deposit. (Currently that's the maximum allowed in some states.) That totals $37,500.

If the owner has simply spent this money as it comes in (hoping to pay back the old tenant's deposit with the deposit from the next tenant), negotiations should deal with how to credit that money to the buyer. Other times, the seller has carefully kept that money in a bank account. Now negotiations center on whether the seller gets to keep it or whether it's transferred to the buyer.

Since the deposits may be a significant part of the cash involved in the sale, it's a big deal point, and very often trade-offs in terms of price and financing can be made with it.

How Do You Negotiate Financing?

The final deal point we'll consider is the financing. It's important to remember that the very best institutional financing in the real estate world goes to owner-occupants of single-family homes. When you're working with an investment property, the financing is much less available and usually at a higher price.

For example, if you're buying an apartment building, strip shopping center, or industrial building(s), you can forget about low-down or nothing-down financing. (Unless you get some of it from the seller.)

TIP

Look for good financing from the lender who handled the construction loan. These lenders will often offer good "take out" or permanent financing in order to assure that a buyer is found for the property and their financing is made secure.

Institutional financing on investment properties may often be only 60 to 75 percent of market value at a variety of interest rates. Thus, if a seller can offer good financing on a project by, for example, carrying back 20 or 30 percent in the form of a second (or third, fourth, or higher) mortgage, the trade-off can often be negotiated into a higher price. Similarly, a buyer who comes in with a lot of cash can often command a much lower price.

Financing in industrial, income, and commercial property is far more critical than it is in housing, and good financing commands far more leverage as a deal point.

The Bottom Line

As I said at the beginning of this chapter, the rules are basically the same when negotiating investment property. The main things that are different are the deal points and the amounts involved.

17

Win the Battle at Closing

During the course of most deals, you will find that at certain times you hold high leverage for negotiating and at other times, low leverage. At the beginning of most real estate transactions, buyers and sellers usually have high cards. They can negotiate price, terms, and all conditions. If they don't like the deal, they can walk away from it with little to lose.

On the other hand, after an escrow has been run, a loan secured, the title cleared, all documents prepared, and the time to close the deal has arrived, the leverage is largely lost. Now, when the buyers or sellers come in on the final day to sign the closing documents, they have very little room to negotiate.

Yes, of course, if they don't like what's presented to them, they can walk away. But, there could be severe penalties for doing so—limited not just to the loss of the deal, but also possibly including a demand for damages from the other party.

In this chapter, we're going to consider negotiating the closing: the time when it's presumably too late to do anything but sign, the time when your leverage has ebbed to the lowest point.

What Can Go Wrong?

First off, let's consider some of the potential pitfalls faced by the *buyers* at closing. It's at this time that buyers first see the actual loan documents they will sign. The lender's HUD-1 statement, which details loan costs, is given to buyers/borrowers only one day before closing. And sometimes, more often than professionals care to admit, the documents don't quite express the terms the buyers originally agreed to, or thought they did. Maybe there's an extra percentage of a point to pay, maybe the interest rate is a tiny bit higher, or maybe there is a list of extra "garbage costs."

TRAP

The Real Estate Settlement Procedures Act (RESPA) is supposed to take care of such problems. As soon as you apply for a mortgage, the lender is required to issue you a preliminary statement telling you what your costs will be. This supposedly assures you that there won't be horrendous surprise changes at closing. If changes are necessary, a new statement must be issued. But interest rates and points do fluctuate during the time a transaction is being consummated. Lenders often estimate costs based on industry standards, which can sometimes be far off reality. A few lenders simply disregard their original estimates. And sometimes buyers just don't pay attention to all those extra costs mentioned in the preliminary statement. In short, while RESPA has helped avoid the huge surprises previously sprung on buyers at closing, many small surprises still do slip through.

From a *seller's* perspective, the closing can also be a shock. Maybe the seller never did carefully add up all the costs that were going to come out of the sale of the property. These can include the real estate agent's commission, pay off of existing financing, proration of taxes and insurance, termite inspection and repair, document fees, title and escrow charges, and maybe a dozen others. Sometimes happy sellers waltz into the escrow office only to have their day ruined when they realize that the amount they actually will receive from the sale is significantly less than what they had anticipated.

What Can You Do to Avoid Closing Problems?

Sometimes the best negotiating tack is to be alert. A lot of closing problems can be avoided simply by anticipation early on. For the buyer, it's important to carefully read the RESPA statement and question any cost at the time you learn of it. That's when the closing process is just beginning and there's still time to switch lenders. Also, get in writing the actual loan commitment in terms of interest rate, points, and costs. If you're dealing with a reputable lender, the company will often stand behind any "mistakes" or low quotes that one of its employees made. But only if you've got it in writing.

As a *buyer*, if you wait until closing and want to negotiate a problem with a lender, you basically have no leverage at all. You can yell and scream and holler that you'll complain to the Federal Trade Commission and the state real estate licensing department. But although these agencies might act if they receive enough complaints against an individual lender, their action probably will come months or years too late to help you. The lender knows it's sitting fat and pretty and may simply refuse to negotiate any changes at all.

Therefore, it's often better to be pleasant and try to negotiate small "misunderstandings" at the closing. Sometimes responsible lenders will take out unnecessary charges.

From the *seller's* perspective, make sure you are aware of the true costs of all items you'll have to pay for out of the sale. You should be able to calculate this down to within a couple of dollars well in advance of closing and negotiate for them early, thus avoiding any nasty surprises at closing.

TIP

Any real estate agent worth his or her salt will prepare a list of costs and present it to the seller before the seller signs the sales agreement. I've seen agents who can present such lists down to within $50 of eventual costs. It's a service that good agents supply as part of their commission fee.

What Do You Do
When Things Go Wrong?

Okay, we've discussed what to do to prevent problems. But what do you do if you didn't pay any attention early on or something unexpected comes up? You walk in to sign the final closing documents and the amount you'll receive is too low or the loan is wrong or there's some other condition that isn't quite right. What can you do about it at this late date?

The answer depends to a large extent on how gutsy a negotiator you are and who can correct the problem. If it's an issue between buyer and seller (not the lender or some other third party), then you actually may have more leverage than you realize.

In most cases (but not all), by the time the deal is ready to close, both buyer and seller are most eager to get things over with. The buyer wants to get the property; the seller wants to get the money; and both have already made moving plans and told friends, relatives, and associates about the deal. Not to go through with the sale now can mean financial as well as emotional distress. In other words, both parties want to make it happen.

Thus, when a buyer or a seller balks at signing the closing documents because of something he or she doesn't like in them, the other party will be greatly upset . . . and may be willing to move mountains to get the deal closed.

For example, the seller walks in, looks at the closing documents, and says in an aggrieved tone, "I'm being charged $1,700 to prorate the taxes on this property. I was distinctly told at the time we signed the sales agreement that my proration costs wouldn't be more than $1,000. It's $700 too high."

The escrow officer (or attorney or whoever is handling the closing) nods sympathetically and says, "You agreed to your prorations when you signed the preliminary escrow documents and the sales agreement. That's the amount it works out to."

The seller takes a strong negotiating position and says, "Nope. I refuse. I'll pay $1,000 and not a penny more. Redraw the documents!"

Now the escrow officer is in a bind. He or she can't change anything unless both parties agree. So the escrow officer gets on the phone and calls the agent (if there is one), who calls the buyer and explains the problem. The agent says, "That crazy seller won't sign because of prorations and is threatening to walk out of the deal over

$700." The buyer is irate, maybe even threatens to sue. The agent explains that's the buyer's right, but then the deal won't close, the buyer won't get the house (at least not right away), and any lawsuit could take years—all over $700. An angry buyer eventually says, "Okay, give him the money, anything to close the deal."

On the other hand, sometimes a party to a transaction will be sneaky and use the closing to get something he or she otherwise couldn't get. Once, for example, I saw a buyer who wanted to get a rather spectacular front porch light included in the sale. (She wanted personal property thrown in with the real property. See Chapter 14.) The sellers refused, saying it had cost them several hundred dollars. They were willing to sell it, but not just give it away. The buyer persisted for a while, but in the end signed the sales agreement sans the lamp.

But then at closing, the buyer refused to sign saying she simply couldn't have the house without the front porch lamp. She wouldn't go through with the deal unless the sellers threw it in. Do you think the sellers were going to lose a sale on the day the deal was to close because of a porch lamp?

TRAP

Beware of threatening to pull out of a transaction at the close. By then, contingencies will presumably have been removed, which means that there may be no legally acceptable reason for you to back out. Your risk is that the other party will be sufficiently angry to refuse to back down, and the whole matter could end up in court—where you could lose. On the other hand, many people will give in when there's a small amount involved just to get the deal over with.

Who Controls the Escrow?

It's important to understand the true function of the escrow officer in negotiations. (It doesn't matter whether it's a company or an individual such as an attorney acting as the escrow officer.) The buyer or the seller who opens the escrow—who sets it up—basically controls it, not the escrow officer. Nevertheless, the escrow officer still plays a crucial role.

The escrow officer often is the one who calls to let you know some action required by the contract hasn't been completed. If he or she delays in calling, the escrow might be delayed by days or even weeks.

The escrow officer is the one who calls for necessary documents. If the documents are called for too early, they may need to be redrawn, causing delays and extra costs. Called for too late, they can cause the deal to sour.

In short, the escrow officer can make the deal go smoothly or can make it drag out. How the process is handled is usually determined by the loyalty of the escrow officer. You want an officer loyal to you. Therefore, try to negotiate the right to open (and thereby help control) escrow.

Who Pays the Escrow Fees?

Besides the commission, there are usually two separate big charges at closing. One is for title insurance, the other is for the escrow. These fees are determined by the escrow company and the title insurance company.

TIP

Fees can vary depending on your state. Some states regulate these fees. Shop around to find the lowest. Also, if the property was sold in the recent past, say the last two years, there may be a big cut in the fees—*if* you ask for it.

Typically, which party pays these fees is a matter of negotiation. Usually, tradition will dictate whether buyer or seller pays (or they split the cost). But you can argue to have the other party pay these costs.

Business is business, and the payment of the escrow fees is negotiable. But if you want the other party to pay, it's best to make it a deal point at the time of negotiating the sales agreement. It's a bit late to do it when escrow is ready to close, although you can force the issue at any time.

Winning the battle at closing is 100 percent adequate preparation and 10 percent guts!

Negotiating Your Way Out of Foreclosure

Foreclosure is not as rare a thing as many people suppose. At any given time, anywhere from 1 to 5 percent of the country's housing stock may be in foreclosure. If you find yourself in this unenviable position, here are some negotiating tips to consider.

What Is the Foreclosure Procedure?

The foreclosure process varies from state to state. But in general it always involves a period of time during which the borrower can make up back payments and correct any default. (*Default* is a technical term that means that the borrower has failed to meet, or has defaulted, on the obligations he or she has under the mortgage.)

After that time period, there is either a judicial foreclosure in which the lender goes to court to secure title to the borrower's home, or a trust deed sale in which the lender uses an independent third party, a trustee, to gain title to the property without going to court. Most states today use the trust deed method because of the speed (as little time as 60 days) and the reduced cost to the lender.

That's the procedure. What's important to realize is that if you're late even one month on your mortgage payment, most lenders will report that to a credit agency and it will appear on your credit

187

record as a late payment. While one late payment usually won't damage your credit too badly (we'll see an exception in a moment), a series of late payments will.

If you stop making payments altogether, and the lender goes through the entire foreclosure process, a report of that will also make its way to a credit agency. The importance of a foreclosure on a credit record cannot be underemphasized. Generally speaking, *no* institutional lender will offer another mortgage to anyone who has had a foreclosure on their record for many years to come.

TRAP

Mortgage lenders are highly sensitive to late mortgage payments. To get the best loans today—generally speaking, Fannie Mae or Freddie Mac underwritten financing (called "conforming" loans)—you cannot have any blemishes on your credit, not even one late mortgage payment.

TIP

Whatever you do, if you ever plan to buy another home, don't let your house go to foreclosure. Borrow to make that payment, sell the property at a loss, but don't let them foreclose. The effect on your credit can be devastating for years to come.

What Can You Do When You're in Default?

Most of us today know of someone who has lost his or her house to foreclosure in the not too distant past. It has become that common. However, here's a story that's been told less often.

Jerry and Pat had just bought a comfortable upscale home in the Los Angeles area that they had stretched to buy. But both had good jobs. However, Jerry was in a high-tech start-up company and, during the dot-com bubble craze, his company went belly up. He could not find other work to fit his job skills, but he kept trying.

Jerry had some severance pay and Pat was still working as a computer programmer for a high-tech company, so they managed to get by and pay all their bills, including their rather hefty mortgage payment. However, about a year after Jerry was laid off, Pat's company closed its doors and she was without work as well. Now they were in a real financial pickle.

For a few months they hung on. But, without Pat's income, they couldn't make that big mortgage payment.

On the first day of the first month that they couldn't make their home payment, Jerry called the lender and asked to talk to someone in their foreclosure department. He explained to a representative of the lender what his predicament was and said he simply did not have enough money to make the loan payment.

The representative checked Jerry and Pat's payment history and saw that they had never been late. He chuckled and noted that the payment wasn't due until the middle of the month. "Don't worry," he told them. "Something will turn up."

Jerry was surprised at the lender's cavalier attitude, so he followed the phone call with a letter explaining his situation. Next, he put the house up for sale. However, they had probably paid too much when they bought and the market just hadn't caught up. (This was in the late 1990s when housing prices were steadily declining in the area.)

Even worse, they had secured 125 percent financing (and used the extra cash to buy furniture) so they now owed more than their house was worth. They didn't have the equity in the property to offer a reduced price or even to pay a real estate agent to sell it for them.

In Default

Jerry didn't get a call from the lender until he was nearly two months overdue on his payment. Then the lender's loan default department called to find out if he knew his payment was late. Had it gotten lost in the mail?

Jerry said he had called earlier and again explained his situation. He was told he'd be called back. Later that day, another representative called to let Jerry know how serious it was to let payments slip. Again, Jerry explained his situation and again he followed up the conversation with a letter.

A few weeks later, Jerry got a letter from the lender saying that it had reported him to a credit bureau for late payments. They wanted to know if he disputed the claim. He responded that he did not, but included a letter of explanation.

Things went on in this manner for nearly five months. Jerry and Pat had their home up for sale "by owner," but had no offers. Then one day Jerry got a call from the lender.

A representative of the lender's, Bill, wanted to know how he was coming along with finding work or selling his house. Jerry told him the sad news. Bill then asked Jerry if he could send him a copy of the listing agreement showing that the house was for sale. He needed it immediately. Jerry said he was selling by owner because of his lack of equity. But he had prepared a flyer describing the property and he sent that to Bill. Two days later, Bill called back and said he'd like a printout from a real estate agent showing comparable sales over the past six months to ascertain that Jerry was pricing his house at market. Jerry immediately called an agent whom he had talked with before and got the agent to send it out.

A week later, Bill called back and wanted proof that Jerry and his wife were really out of work. Jerry did have an old termination slip from his last job and asked if a recent unemployment check to his wife would suffice. Bill said they would.

A week after that, Bill called again and said that if Jerry couldn't make up the payments, the lender would be forced to start formal foreclosure proceedings. That meant that Jerry would lose his home in about four months. Jerry and Pat asked for a meeting.

Facing Foreclosure

At the meeting with Bill, Jerry and Pat explained the situation as they saw it. Their professional fields were depressed at the moment, there was a recession on (at that time), and they had a loan for more than their home was worth.

Then they began formal negotiating. (Keeping the lender abreast of the situation and communicating was a kind of negotiating too.) Yes, the lender could foreclose, but if it did, it would end up with a house it couldn't resell for what had been put into it. As it was, even if Jerry and Pat sold, they wouldn't get any money out of the deal anyway. Then they reiterated, "If the lender foreclosed, it would end up with a house that was worth less than the mortgage amount."

Bill grimaced at that. Then he offered Jerry a proposition. He said the lender would allow him to skip the next three payments if, after that, Jerry made up all the interest on all the payments he had missed. The lender would even offer him a plan of slightly lower payments to help make up what he owed. Bill said the lender would like to extend the loan to make the payments even lower, but since Jerry and Pat had only recently gotten it, there was no way the lender could do that.

Jerry explained that he didn't think he could make up any payments until he found a job. But he would try. They agreed.

Three months later, Jerry's situation hadn't changed and he asked for another meeting with the lender. After he explained his situation, he asked if the lender could simply forget the payments for a longer period of time, say a year or more, until he got back on his feet.

Bill conferred and said they'd get back to him. The next week he was given official notice that the foreclosure proceedings had started. Jerry began to look for another place to live.

A month later, Bill called back. He wanted to know if Jerry had any nibbles on the house. He hadn't. Bill also wanted to know how Jerry's job hunting was progressing. He reported there was no luck there either.

By the end of the next month, Jerry and Pat had made arrangements to move to her family's home in another state. Hopefully, they both would get a better start there. Jerry called the lender one last time and asked for a conference.

When Bill met with him, Jerry pointed out that there was no way he could make up the back payments, now totaling nearly 11 months. Further, since the house was still worth less than the mortgage amount (if a buyer could be found at any price in this market), there was no way he could sell.

However, it would be two more months before the lender could complete foreclosure according to the rules in his state. Further, Jerry had maintained the house well during that time and it was in great condition right now. At this point, Jerry upped the ante.

He said that if the lender persisted in seeking foreclosure, Jerry would simply "walk." Chances are the house would be vandalized and it might cost the lenders many thousands to put it back in shape. Plus, there was always the cost of completing the foreclosure process.

However, if the lender would accept a "deed in lieu of foreclosure," Jerry would transfer the property to the lender immediately. Then the lender could try selling the property itself, perhaps with more luck since it might offer much better terms (financing) than Jerry could.

TIP

A *deed in lieu of foreclosure* simply means that the lender accepts title to the property without going through the foreclosure process. For Jerry, it meant no record of foreclosure would appear on his credit report. However, a notice of getting a "deed in lieu" would show up. It was, however, a lesser bad credit mark.

The lender's representative, Bill, considered and said he'd get back to Jerry. He did the next day and agreed. A "deed in lieu" was drawn up and Jerry was out from under.

A "Deed in Lieu of Foreclosure"

While offering a "deed in lieu of foreclosure" is much better, from a credit perspective, than having a foreclosure on the records, it's still not wonderful. Jerry's credit record still noted months of non-payment. And today many mortgage lenders ask in their application if a would-be borrower has ever given a "deed in lieu." An answer of, "Yes" might still mean no new mortgage. However, a "Yes" accompanied by a letter of explanation plus several years of good credit might indeed secure a new loan—because there was no foreclosure on the record. In short, foreclosure is the worst possible way to lose a house. A "deed in lieu of foreclosure" shows an effort was made by the borrower to protect credit. It's far, far better than foreclosure.

The Key to Negotiating Out of Foreclosure

The single most important point to understand in this example is that Jerry and Pat constantly communicated with the lender. Communication was the key to their ability to get payments delayed and then get an alternative to foreclosure. Consider that if Jerry had never called the lender, had simply ignored the lender's calls to him (which, unfortunately, is what most borrowers in default do), the lender would simply have written Jerry and Pat off as a lost cause. It would immediately have started foreclosure and pursued it to the end. In other words, the lender would have seen no alternative but to take the harshest possible course of action. Jerry carefully presented it with a better alternative.

TIP

Lenders don't want to foreclose on homes. Once a lender takes a property back, it becomes a liability instead of an asset. A lender would much rather give the borrower every possible opportunity to hang onto the house or get out from under by selling.

But once the lender began foreclosure, Jerry wasn't hesitant about taking a tough posture, namely to threaten to "walk" and potentially allow the house to receive thousands of dollars of vandalism.

What You Can Negotiate from a Lender

Lenders may be willing to do one or more of the following:

- Restructure the mortgage by extending the term so that you have lower payments, so long as the lender does not ultimately lose any interest
- Temporarily allow you to miss payments until you get back on your feet by adding interest not paid onto the loan amount

- Completely forgive interest and payments for up to a year or more, so long as you can demonstrate that you have the potential to pick up payments once again after that time
- Take back the property "in lieu of foreclosure" so that your credit does not have a foreclosure showing up on it

TIP

A big question is whether or not the loan is conforming. Remember, a "conforming" loan originally conformed to the underwriter's parameters, the underwriters usually being quasi-government secondary market lenders such as Fannie Mae or Freddie Mac. These lenders generally insist that the primary lender make every effort (such as reducing or forgiving some payments) to help the borrower get out of default.

When it comes to foreclosure, however, a lender is restricted in what it can offer a desperate borrower by other underwriter guidelines. However, those guidelines have been so liberalized in recent years that they are very close to the above description. A portfolio lender (for example, a bank or S&L that made the loan out of its own funds) might be even more liberal.

What You Can Do to Have a Better Negotiating Posture

- Keep in touch. Immediately reply to any calls or letters from the lender, no matter when they come. Never let calls go unanswered.
- Try to get out from under the mortgage by selling the property.
- Clearly show the lender that your financial condition is such that you have no way to make the payments. This could mean being willing to send the lender, at any moment, bank statements, unemployment records, or anything else demanded. You can't be too finicky about keeping your finances private when you're faced with foreclosure as a real possibility.

- Make suggestions to the lender about how you would like the matter handled. If you think you could get back on your feet if you had a vacation from payments, present that as an offer. Just be sure that you have a good reason why you'd be in better financial condition later and know exactly how long it will take. If you realize that you can't get out, consider a "deed in lieu of foreclosure."

- When the time is right, don't hesitate to leverage your position by threatening to walk away from the problem.

What's important is to present yourself as doing everything possible to get out of the mortgage problem you're in. It's not that lenders are sympathetic to your position, although those in the lender's employment may surely be. It's that you have to make the lender see that you have no other alternatives and that what you're proposing to the lender is better for it than foreclosure.

TRAP

Don't try the sympathy approach. Mortgage lenders don't cry, and they really don't care about you. What they want are performing loans. Barring that, they want the cheapest, surest financial method of solving the problem you are presenting. Offer them a viable solution and chances are they'll take it.

If you try negotiating your way out of foreclosure and make a dedicated effort, you could be pleasantly surprised at the results.

Index

About the Author

Robert Irwin is one of America's foremost experts in every area of real estate. He is the author of McGraw-Hill's Tips and Traps series, as well as *The Home Buyer's Checklist, How to Get Started in Real Estate Investing,* and *How to Buy a Home When You Can't Afford It.*